CLONE YOURSELF

BUILD A TEAM THAT UNDERSTANDS YOUR VISION, SHARES YOUR PASSION, AND RUNS YOUR BUSINESS FOR YOU

W0010442

JEFF HILDERMAN

Disclaimer:

The advice and strategies found within may not be suitable for every situation. This work is sold with the understanding that neither the author nor the publisher are held responsible for the results accrued from the advice in this book.

Copyright © 2017 Jeff Hilderman. All rights reserved.

No portion of this book may be reproduced, stored in a retrieval system, or transmitted in any form or by any means — electronic, mechanical, photocopying, recording, scanning, or other — except for brief quotations in critical reviews or articles, without the prior written permission of the publisher.

ISBN-13: 978-1-7750383-3-7

DEDICATION

To my parents, Greg and Diane, who have always stood in my corner and unconditionally supported my endeavors. Your family values and personal sacrifices have made me the person I am today. Thank you for everything.

To my in-laws, Richard and Donna, thank you for your mentorship and encouragement. I would certainly not stand where I am without you, and I'll be forever grateful for your trust, kindness, and generosity.

To my children, Hannah, Leo, and Bailey, thank you for always showing me the sunny side of life. You're the reason why I get up every morning and do what I do.

And lastly, I'd like to dedicate this book to my wife, Tasha, as none of this would be possible without her support. Thank you for doing double parent duty during the early mornings, late nights, and weekends. Thank you for putting up with my lengthy conversations and crazy ideas. And most importantly, thank you for sharing this life with me – I'm the luckiest guy in the world!

CLAIM YOUR FREE AUDIOBOOK

To thank you for purchasing my book,

I would like to give you the Audiobook version for **FREE!**

DOWNLOAD YOUR COPY AT:

www.jeffhilderman.com/audiobook

DOWNLOAD YOUR FREE WORKBOOK

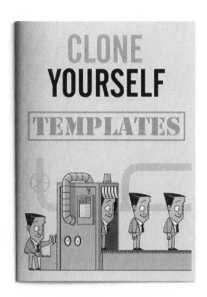

I'm all about the quick wins! Save yourself the hassle and download the templates found in this book for **FREE!**

DOWNLOAD YOUR WORKBOOK AT:

www.jeffhilderman.com/resources

CONTENTS

Section Three

DEVELOPING YOUR CLONE

Section Four

LETTING GO

Section Five

IGNITING YOUR PASSION

Chapter 1

CONNECTING THE DOTS

Why do some entrepreneurs seem to have more time, energy, and focus than everyone else? Given the same number of hours in a day and similar abilities and challenges, what are they doing differently to scale their companies so quickly? Where do they find the time to plan for the future when the rest of us are too busy stamping out fires and controlling chaos? Who are these crazy people and what makes them so special? What's the big secret? These are the types of questions that plagued me for years – questions that needed answers.

THE PROBLEM

After completing my second year of university, I was burned out and needed a break. As my friends competed for a handful of summer jobs offering invaluable industry experience, I opted for sunshine and exercise at a local home improvement center. It was there that I met my wife, who also happened to be the owner's daughter (another story for another time). She worked alongside her parents, two sisters, and brother, all of whom were actively involved in the business.

Despite the razzing I received from my comrades in the lumberyard, I was graciously welcomed into her family's inner circle and exposed to an entirely new and exciting world of a family-run business. I was hooked! To make a long story short, I graduated 4 years later, got married and accepted a sales position within their organization.

Fast-forward fifteen years. I was a Vice-President, had earned my stripes and had the battle scars to prove it. Our business exploded in growth and received numerous awards along the way. But there was a problem: we were putting in ridiculously long hours and burning the candle at both ends. Throw three kids into the mix and needless to say, my hands were full (both figuratively and literally). I needed help.

In that time, I read more business books than I could count and attended scores of seminars to improve my skills as a leader, husband, and father. But my achievements were often short-lived, and I began to question if there was something wrong with me. After all, the experts had done their job so the onus must be on me. My frustration grew, along with my list of unanswered questions. Then I had an epiphany. Well actually, two.

One morning I rummaged through my desk and stumbled across an old notebook. Inside were the notes from a roundtable meeting I had attended earlier in the year, outlining the typical problems my colleagues and I had grown accustomed to complaining about every time we met. I skimmed over the action plan and thought to myself, "I don't have time for this," and as I motioned to return my book to the drawer, it hit me – why didn't I have time? What was holding me back?

Suddenly the problem was obvious. My long-standing issue wasn't the result of faulty advice, but rather with my ability to implement it. I couldn't move forward because I was stuck dealing with all sorts of random things in the business. I also realized I wasn't alone, and many of my colleagues were in similar predicaments.

There was a missing link between destinations A and B, and it became my mission to find out what it was. So instead of picking up another self-help book, I focused my attention on what my role models were doing rather than what they were saying.

THE SOLUTION

As it turns out these entrepreneurs, the ones who seem to have unlimited time and resources, are no different than you or me. We all have the same ambitions for success, the freedom of choice, and the technical abilities to achieve great things in our respective fields.

However, unlike the masses, they've also developed a specific skill set attributed to their expedited growth. The good news is that it can be taught to anyone at any stage of their business. For those who've learned how to clone themselves, the future is wide open and filled with endless possibilities.

Simply put, **cloning yourself is the act of working yourself out of a job**. This goes beyond the conventional understanding of hiring employees and delegating tasks. Instead, cloning yourself is about instilling your vision, your drive, your philosophies and your strategic mindset into others who have the ability to carry the torch forward.

The problem with delegation is that it only works when you have the right people, doing the right things, the right way; and when you don't, everything inevitably funnels its way back to you. This is why so many entrepreneurs hit a wall and become the bottleneck of their business. They fall into the daily grind of stamping out fires and doing everything themselves because they're unable to effectively delegate to their team.

Cloning yourself solves this problem. Remember, the goal is to work yourself out of a job. So instead of delegating tasks, you will focus on attracting, developing and leading the right people, to do those right things, the right way. Consequently, you'll not only have somebody to delegate the small picture to, but the big picture as well.

Imagine that your business is running itself. You have no obligations, deadlines, urgent emails or paperwork– nothing. The only thing on your desk is a notebook with a handful of minor things to follow up on. Otherwise, you're free to do as much or as little as you please.

You decide to take a walk and greet your team, who eagerly bring you up to speed on the day's events. Potential problems have already been resolved, new opportunities pursued, and everyone is working together like a well-oiled machine. Sound pretty good? So how do you turn this dream into a reality?

This is what I learned: **Every business has a tipping point where it's no longer feasible for you to be the immediate person in charge.** Those who figure this out will continue to expand on their success, while those who don't will eventually plateau and spin their wheels indefinitely.

Entrepreneurs wear many hats and the end game should be to give them all away. Your team will always need guidance, motivation and feedback to get the job done correctly and on time. And while these are all necessary duties of a leader, that doesn't mean they must be performed by you.

While I will use the term *your clone* to describe the person who will eventually lead in your stead, the strategies in this book are applicable for every position so you can eventually build your dream team.

I share my story because I know exactly how it feels to not have all the answers. To drift aimlessly without a clear direction and purpose; to operate on a different wavelength from the rest of your team. I've experienced first hand the struggles of getting your plans to fly and staying motivated in the presence of adversity.

I also know the challenges of balancing a personal and professional life. The pressure to be everything, to everyone all the time. The sacrifices we make to chase our dreams, and the decisions we have to live with. I wrote this book because I believe entrepreneurship should be exciting and rewarding, not a burden.

Clone Yourself is the solution for anyone plagued by the *Entrepreneur's Curse*, those who've become their own best employee and are stuck working *in* their business instead of working *on* it. It's your comprehensive guide to attract, develop and lead your dream team so you can finally create a business and a life you love! Here's how we'll do it.

THE GAME PLAN

Before we jump right into the cloning process, we have to make sure you're sufficiently prepared for the challenge. The reality is that this program, specifically the first thirty days, is going to be tough. I won't sugarcoat it and neither should you. It's going to take time away from all of your other responsibilities, life will get in the way, and at times, you'll be ready to throw in the towel.

But don't worry, I've got you covered!

The first section is all about getting your head in the game. We'll begin with your mindset, discuss the fundamental concepts of time management, examine the qualities of an effective leader, and determine your leadership style. Upon completion, you'll have a renewed sense of purpose and be sufficiently prepared to embark on your journey toward real, long-term change.

In Section Two, we'll cover all of the big picture stuff, including organizational culture, vision and mission statements, core values, performance standards, job descriptions, and branding. Even if you've done this before, now will be the time to re-evaluate it and make sure it represents the best version of you. We are dedicating a full thirty days to this section for a reason, so don't breeze through it. What happens here will dictate everything else moving forward, so it's essential to get everything out of your head and on to paper.

Likewise, if you're worried that thirty days won't be long enough, that's ok too. At this point, done is better than perfect, and there will be plenty of time to go back and make improvements. After all, this is what working on your business is all about. Hold yourself accountable to the deadline and do whatever is needed to stay on track. All of this is designed to challenge your brain, so when your head begins to hurt, you know you're doing it right.

Section Three is where you'll put everything into practice. We'll go through a systematic procedure to hire, train, and support your clone, and provide all of the tools you'll need to bring them up to speed in thirty days' time.

Section Four will mark the final leg of the program, with a comprehensive look at how to benchmark your clone's success, set future goals, and employ strategies to sustain long-term success for both of you. The final section is the icing on the cake, where we'll take a look at what your future has in store. Ready? Here we go!

Section One

THE FUNDAMENTALS

Chapter 2

RESET YOUR MINDSET

We all know a Debbie Downer, the person who is constantly a victim of circumstance and can never get ahead in life. She is consumed with negativity, loves to complain, makes excuses, and points out problems instead of solutions. The sky is falling for Debbie, and she always seems to be at the epicenter of drama.

And then there's Sunshine Suzy, who brightens any room she walks into. Her positivity is contagious and she exudes confidence with a smile on her face, and her head held high. Suzy is grounded, proactive, and listens to understand rather than to respond. She cares about the people around her and takes an interest in their personal lives.

So, who do you think will be more successful in life, Debbie or Suzy?

Our mindset is the lens in which we view ourselves and the world around us. It filters the information we send and receive, influences our decisions, and affects how others perceive us. But most importantly, our mindset determines how far we go in life and the impact we leave behind.

It's human nature to take the path of least resistance. Whether we're trying to lose weight, quit smoking or save money, it's all too easy to revert to our old ways. Why? Because doing the hard things in life is well...hard! But if you're serious about changing your ways for good, the first order of business is to shift your mindset and mentally prepare yourself for the journey that lies ahead.

So forget about the past, forget the present, and don't worry about the future. Just clear your mind, and let's begin with a clean slate.

LET IT GO

There's a big difference between having a bad day and having a bad attitude. Even the most enthusiastic people are allowed to feel frustrated and discouraged– it's a part of being human. But what separates the optimists from the trolls under the bridge is their willingness to take responsibility for their actions.

It's easy and downright tempting to complain and make excuses, but rarely does anything good come out of it. Think about the last time you were trapped in a room with a chronically negative person. Was it an uplifting experience or could you feel the goodness of your soul being sucked out of you?

Misery loves company, but your attitude is always a choice. You can either practice self-control and consciously choose when to open the pressure relief valve, or remain in a reactive state and reside in despair– just like Debbie Downer.

For the record, I'm not suggesting you bottle up your emotions. It's perfectly healthy to acknowledge your feelings and release residual tension, but doing it in the right place at the right time is key. Schedule a hard, ugly cry on your drive home from work. Treat yourself to a hot bath and a glass (or two) of wine. Meditate, hit the gym, or do whatever works for you. Just remember the pity party ends at midnight and tomorrow is a new day.

Forgiveness is the epitome of letting go. Mistakes will happen and when they do, we can either beat ourselves up and throw in the towel, or choose to forgive ourselves and learn from the experience. Likewise, when we give ourselves permission to fail, we're more inclined to step outside of our comfort zone and take calculated risks.

Forgiving others, however, presents additional challenges and is the true test of character. Think about your last runaway argument, where an isolated incident quickly escalated out of control. When facts and opinions were replaced with speculation and insults, and both parties were focused on staging their next counterattack instead of working toward a resolution. At least half the time these showdowns end with hurt feelings and compounded problems.

In these circumstances, we tend to hold out for the coveted "You're right, and I'm sorry," instead of having the courage to be the first one to extend the olive branch. This doesn't justify the actions of others or nullify your feelings, it is simply the decision to move forward and choose reconciliation over your pride.

The path to forgiveness begins with empathy and accepting the shortcomings in people. We're all guilty of judging others to some degree, especially when we're left disappointed. We believe the situation unfolded because "he doesn't care" or "she's not trustworthy," attacking their character instead of accepting their flaws.

Ironically, when the tables are turned, we are more likely to excuse our own actions and link them to external factors beyond our control. We let ourselves off the hook because the alarm wasn't set, or we were swamped at work. In other words, we're more lenient with ourselves than we are with others.

In reality, most people are good. They have dreams, want to be successful and to be recognized for a job well done. We live in a selfish world, but we can all do our part to make it a better place.

As friends, family, colleagues, and mentors, let's focus on building other people up and supporting them in both good times and bad. Take an interest in their lives, have meaningful conversations and don't sweat the small stuff. Putting yourself in somebody else's shoes is the best way to appreciate their struggles and forgive grievances.

Positivity comes from within, and life's too short to be anything but happy. So ask yourself, are challenges seen as obstacles or opportunities? Are mistakes setbacks or learning experiences? Do misunderstandings equate to conflict or resolution?

The key to letting go of negativity lies in our willingness to change our perspective and be proactive. It's with this mindset that we're able to persevere through difficult times and help others to do the same. Positivity is contagious, but it has to start with you.

NO MORE EXCUSES...SERIOUSLY

We make excuses all the time for a variety of reasons, mostly as a defense mechanism to protect ourselves from humiliation and criticism. Nobody wants to be cast in a negative light, so if there's an opportunity to shift the blame without consequence, the decision seems obvious. Again, this all comes back to letting ourselves off the hook and deflecting accountability. It might be convenient, but it won't get you very far in life.

The same can be said for procrastination. Consider all the reasons why you put something off. You're tired and would rather do the work another day. You're afraid of what others might think if you don't succeed. You don't have all the answers, and that scares you. But this isn't what we tell ourselves. Instead, we rationalize that it isn't the right time to proceed with our plans.

Anyone who says they don't have enough time for something is full of baloney. Every single one of us is busy with whatever occupies our life. Doctors are busy with their patients; parents are busy with their kids, and teenagers are busy with their friends. When we say we're too busy for something, what we're actually saying is we aren't willing to find the time or make the necessary sacrifices.

There's plenty of free time each day; it just might be occupied by something else of less importance: Breaks at work, watching television, sleeping in, recreational sports and hobbies, the list goes on and on. This, of course, is *your time* and you're free to spend it as you wish, but claiming that you are too busy is a lousy excuse. If it matters, make it a priority and schedule it into your day.

Failing is part of the success story, but unfortunately, some people don't stick around long enough to figure this out. They get discouraged, quit, and justify their actions with excuses, having never learned that giving up on their dreams was a result of giving up on themselves.

If something doesn't work out, go back to the drawing board and figure it out. Conduct research, experiment or bring in extra help if needed. When things feel like they're spiraling out of control, push the pause button and take a step back to look at the bigger picture.

Sometimes we can lose sight of the original problem when the simplest solution is right under our nose. If you need to strengthen your knowledge, do it. If you need more experience, then practice, practice, practice! Improvement comes from repetition, not getting it perfect the first time. Do whatever you need to do, just don't make excuses– they're dream-killers.

The only difference between the impossible and the possible is your mindset. We have access to virtually all the world's data at the click of a button. We can travel between continents in a matter of hours instead of weeks. We're seeing medical breakthroughs to remedy conditions once considered fatal. Less than a century ago, these ideas were inconceivable and deemed impossible, and yet with hard work and perseverance, these dreams, like so many others, have become a reality. There will always be reasons not to do something, but don't let them prevent you from accomplishing great things.

KEEP THE END IN MIND

There's a consensus in the athletic community that competitions are won well in advance during training. The victor's success is no doubt attributed to their hard work and determination, but all of this begins with a clear vision.

Olympians train for years for the opportunity to stand on the podium with a gold medal around their neck. Body builders subject themselves to grueling diet and exercise regimens to sculpt themselves to perfection. Regardless of the sport, every athlete in training is an athlete 24/7. They're able to push through the pain and make incredible sacrifices because they never lose sight of their vision.

With any goal, believing in yourself is half the battle. Consider how many New Year resolutions you've made over the years. How did your motivation in June compare to January? I'm assuming not very well. Conventional wisdom tells us things get easier over time, and while true in principle, the fine print should read *in the presence of motivation.*

For example, my kids loved building cushion forts and block castles. Without hesitation, they'd rebuild them over and over until they got it just right, or until frustration got the better of them. When I sensed it was getting to this point, I'd offer a few words of encouragement and sometimes a helping hand. This was often enough to restore their motivation and recalibrate their focus to the task at hand. My excitement became theirs, and before long, they were tearing it down to start again.

It's the same thing at work when employees are developing new skills. We often forget how uncomfortable and frustrating it can be to learn something new, especially with somebody looking over your shoulder, so as leaders, it's our job to ward off discouragement and build their confidence during this process. Don't underestimate the power of a "good job" or "keep trying" – it can literally be the difference between success and failure.

Think of your goals as little seeds freshly planted in a pot of soil. In the beginning, they're extremely vulnerable to the outside elements and must be continuously nurtured. Over time, the plant establishes firm roots in the soil, becomes hearty and requires less personal attention to survive. But what happens if you stop watering the plant altogether? At first, it becomes stressed and withers, but with a little water, it will make a full recovery. However, continual neglect will eventually kill the plant, regardless of how strong it was.

Goals, like plants, need regular nourishment to flourish. Our motivation is what allows us to rise above our insecurities and persevere through adversity. Hard work is hard, but it's easier to endure when you're focused on the bigger picture.

CHECK YOUR EGO AT THE DOOR

You can't do everything yourself, nor be everything to everyone – this is a fact of life. As leaders, we naturally feel compelled to help as many people as possible, and consequently, bite off more than we can chew. While our heart is in the right place, we may, in fact, be doing more harm than good.

We spend more time solving problems than asking questions. We do things ourselves to ensure the work is done correctly and on time. We manage people instead of systems and keep communication a one-way street. Before we know it, the day is over, and we're frustrated that nobody shares our vision. Go figure.

The first step to solving any problem is to acknowledge it, which in this case is you! It's your responsibility to grow the business, not your ego.

If you're the type of person who loves a good power trip, you'll want to reconsider your approach or forever lose your staff. Pounding fists, making demands, and overriding decisions are the easiest ways to turn people off. Your team is here to help you, but if they don't feel valued, they'll move on to greener pastures. Employees who are externally motivated by fear are only working for themselves; they'll do the bare minimum to get by and couldn't care less about your vision. An organizational culture exhibiting *me* versus *we* is as toxic as it gets.

The same can be said about the control freaks, except they're doing the work instead of demanding results. The interactions between the leader and their employees are certainly more civil, but there's still an absence of trust in the relationship. It might feel good in the beginning to be needed and to solve everyone's problems, but the novelty quickly wears off when more time is spent putting out fires and doing work that isn't your own.

Taking tasks away from your team also sends the wrong message. It may sound in your head like, "I'll take care of this for you," but what you're implying is, "You're not qualified to do this." At first, your employees might not think twice about it, but eventually, they'll lose interest and become disengaged drones floating through the day without a care in the world.

Too much trust can be equally dangerous, especially without the appropriate checks and balances in place. While empowering a self-reliant team is a winning strategy (and the premise of this book), it only works when the organizational culture is fully understood and lived day-to-day. But letting go of the steering wheel doesn't mean removing your hand from the company's pulse altogether.

You may understand the needs of your customers, partners, and team, but can you say with confidence that they're all being met? Are the actions of every single employee aligned with the company's vision and values? Do you know what your customers are *really* saying about you? If you can't answer these questions with conviction, you may have your head in the clouds.

Great leaders put the spotlight on their team instead of themselves. They place the needs of others ahead of their own self-interests and are committed to helping each person reach their full potential. But what makes these leaders truly exceptional is their ability to recognize when their assistance is required and when it's not. They understand that a well-trained and self-motivated team can move mountains and choose to channel this energy, rather than oppress it. So take care of your team, and they'll take care of you.

* * *

Getting into the right mindset is all about finding your zen; that sweet spot in your mind where you feel energized, confident in your abilities and laser-focused on your objective. Positivity is the name of the game, and as the leader, it's your duty to lead by example. Make peace with yourself when things don't go as planned and forgive others for being human. Own up to mistakes and use them to your advantage. Build your team up and give them every opportunity to be successful. That's all this is, just a mental game with yourself.

Learning to clone yourself is as easy or as difficult as you make it. If you're reluctant to change, then I'm sorry to say that your fate is already sealed. But if you're open-minded and willing to do whatever it takes to see this through to the end, then you've already taken your first steps forward. There are no shortcuts and no days off, but keep the end in mind and look forward to what's waiting for you on the other side.

Chapter 3

TIME: USE IT OR LOSE IT

Time is the gift of opportunity, enabling us to experience the world and enrich the lives of others. It interweaves our personal and professional lives so harmoniously that achieving the right balance can be a serious challenge in itself. Nobody wants to choose between a work crisis and a family obligation, which is why learning how to become a time management master is an essential skill for everyone.

In the age of breakfast sandwiches and bedtime emails, we've inadvertently become slaves to ourselves. We feel naked without our smart devices and seize every opportunity to catch up on the latest news, scores, and celebrity gossip. We spend more time on social media than we do physically interacting with loved ones, and even then, we aren't fully present in the moment. We've replaced focused work with mediocre multitasking, working longer and harder with a minimal sense of accomplishment. Worst of all, this has become the new way of doing things and the quality of our life has deteriorated without notice.

We wear multiple hats as employers, mentors, coaches, volunteers, friends and family, so naturally the demands for our personal time are high. Filtering requests and juggling obligations is no easy feat, but there is hope amidst the chaos. In the next four chapters, I'll discuss the time management fundamentals needed to effectively lead a team, including the common time-wasters standing in your way to becoming a productivity powerhouse.

CRUNCHING THE NUMBERS

Time is a blank check, and its value is up to us. We can either leverage it to our advantage or let it slip through our fingers and go to waste. For example, the average person works eight hours per day or eight man-hours. Now imagine the same person led a team of just three people:

One-Man Army: 1 person x 8 hours = **8 Man-Hours**

3 Person Team: 3 people x 8 hours = **24 Man-Hours**

As you can see, the leader could gain up to twenty-four man-hours of productivity every single day! Extrapolate the data to a team of ten, fifty or one hundred people, and the results are pretty staggering. If you also consider that the leader's time has now been repurposed for more meaningful work, such as growing the company and improving efficiencies, the return on investment is even higher. In other words, compounding your productivity is the ticket to exponential growth.

Shifting gears from me to we is the pivotal moment when individuals with good ideas become leaders with a vision. They ascend to a higher level of productivity by first recognizing the true value of their time and where it's best invested. But leveling up doesn't just happen; it involves reassessing your priorities and abandoning comfortable routines for more disciplined structure.

TIME JOURNALING

Time management begins with an understanding of where your time is consumed and why. It's easy to recall the highs and lows of your day, but the most valuable information is what happened in between. Time journaling is useful for capturing a snapshot of your life and identifying the distractions which often go unnoticed. With this information, you'll be more conscious of your actions, and in turn, exercise better judgment.

When I look back at all the strategies I've employed to become a better leader, I'd have to say that auditing my time was one of the best things I ever did. When I first learned about this exercise, I rolled my eyes and quickly dismissed the benefits of an internal audit.

But I went along with it anyway, and was shocked by the frequency of disruption in my day; I'm not talking about emails or phone calls either, I mean people physically standing at my door with a question or concern. I don't recall the exact number, but it was about every fifteen minutes!

Even more interesting was that the majority of interruptions were minor clarifications or confirmations. Initially, I was annoyed by the revolving door in my office, but on paper, it was a clear indication that I needed to spend more time on the sales floor. These disruptions were valid but also controllable, and by making more rounds throughout the day, my team anticipated regular opportunities to touch base and therefore withheld their questions until they saw me.

Within a few short weeks, I had managed to reduce these types of disruptions by almost 90% – pretty amazing if you ask me!

I've journaled my time on numerous occasions over the years, and I'll admit that I always discover something new. I've caught myself spending too much time on non-priority projects and taking on work that I shouldn't. I've had to face the cold, hard truth many times on where I was failing as a leader. I'm also guilty of moving too quickly from project to project without fully analyzing the results.

The point is that you don't really know what's going on until you start writing everything down. Things move quickly, and a lot of your reactions are both instinctive and difficult to recall. Time journaling has not only helped me become a better leader but also trained me to view my own actions through a different lens.

Step 1: Create A Log

First, determine the best medium that works for you. Some people like to use a journal or notebook, while others like myself prefer to use software like Excel or Google Docs (free) so the documents can be saved for referral.

Next, create a log by dividing your day into one-hour intervals from the time you wake up until the time you go to bed.

TIME-WIZARD TIP!

Save yourself the hassle and download this template at www.jeffhilderman.com/resources

Step 2: Start Writing

Fill out your log every hour, including any personal activities, such as exercise, hobbies, travel, eating, and sleeping. Avoid generalizations like "meeting" or "paperwork" because this doesn't provide sufficient insight into where your time was spent. At the end of your first day, your journal should look something like this:

Time Journal: Day 1	
Time	**Activity**
7:00 AM	Woke Up – Slept 8 Hours
8:00 AM	Got ready, ate breakfast and checked email
9:00 AM	Drove to work and responded to messages
10:00 AM	Reviewed reports, phone call with customer
11:00 AM	Coffee break – 15 min, returned 2 phone calls
12:00 PM	Lunch & went for a walk in park
1:00 PM	Checked emails and visited with sales team
2:00 PM	Dealt with upset customer & made new schedule
3:00 PM	Meeting with vendor to review new catalogues
4:00 PM	Meeting 45 min, checked email
5:00 PM	Dropped off brochures to customer, travelled home
6:00 PM	Ate supper and watched the playoffs
7:00 PM	Watched the playoffs
8:00 PM	Watched the playoffs
9:00 PM	Read and go to bed

It's crucial to stick to the schedule, so nothing is forgotten. Set a timer, write yourself a sticky note, or whatever else will keep you on track, just DO NOT wait until the end of the day to fill everything out.

Step 3: Repeat

Continue to log your activities for the next two days, but this time in thirty-minute intervals. Yes, this will feel tedious and distracting, but it's an essential part of the analytical process. Smaller time samples increase the accuracy of your journal and are more likely to identify the interruptions and time-wasters we're looking for.

BONUS POINTS!

Highlight every interruption at work for a greater impact! Even better, use a different colour for each type of distraction.

Step 4: Analyze the Data

So what did you discover after three days of journaling?

- o   How often were you focused on your work and on the right things?
- o   How often were you preoccupied with other people's work?
- o   What were your biggest time-wasters?
- o   When were you busiest and when did you have holes in your day?
- o   Did you pre-plan your day or go with the flow?
- o   Did you set daily goals and hold yourself accountable?
- o   How did you manage paperwork, phone calls, email, and appointments?
- o   Can you identify anything important that was neglected?
- o   If you had to free up two hours of your day, what could be delegated?

Think objectively about your answers, write them down and take the time to digest the information. Hopefully, you weren't too surprised by your findings and can point out where your time is best utilized and wasted. There might even be a few eye-openers that caught you off guard, and quite frankly, that's a good thing.

Acknowledging your inefficiencies can be a tough pill to swallow, but it's also a prerequisite for corrective action. With a newfound perspective on what's happening in your day, you can now take matters into your own hands by protecting your time and redirecting your focus onto the things that matter.

Chapter 4

PROTECTING YOUR TIME

When it comes to managing our time, the road to Hell is paved with good intentions. We want to be helpful, so we take on the work. We want to resolve problems, so we take on the work. We want to avoid conflict, so we take on the work. Even when we know we shouldn't, we take on the work.

Losing control of your day can feel like being stranded on a sinking ship. But remember, the best way to keep a ship from sinking is to plug the hole. In the spur of the moment we may instinctively reach for a bucket to shovel out the water, but until the hole is repaired, we're just working against ourselves and delaying the inevitable. Likewise, with time management, working harder and longer doesn't address the problem of taking on the work that doesn't belong to us. So before we can tighten up our day, we must cut off all unnecessary work at the source.

THE ART OF SAYING NO

Learning to say no is the best way to protect your time, and is a tool frequently used by industry leaders. The goal: to shield yourself from daily distractions without coming off as rude. The end game is to train your team how to think for themselves, solve their own problems, and stay focused without intervention.

You can expect this to feel slightly awkward at first, but with practice, they'll come around. Here are five strategies you can use right now to begin saying no, without actually saying no.

Refusing to solve other people's problems is the most logical place to start, but be forewarned, your employees are cleverer than you think. They know you have the most skin in the game and that you'll instinctively jump in to solve problems and minimize collateral damage. They also know how to manipulate you and disguise their requests as stories and throwaway comments – so pay attention and don't get roped in!

Consider how you'd respond to the following statements:

Talk about opening up a can of worms! These situations often feel like a double-edged sword because on one side, we're concerned for the person and the residual effects on the company, while on the other, we're trying to protect our time and train our staff to become self-reliant. So how do you get your cake and eat it too? It's quite simple actually, and the best part is that the outcome has two winners.

Imagine somebody walks into your office with a puppy (representing their specific problem) and sets it down on your desk. You are free to look at the puppy, touch the puppy and have a discussion about the puppy, but when the conversation ends, the puppy must leave with its owner.

Once the floodgates are open and everything's on the table, it's your job to ensure they leave feeling supported and inspired to take action. The best way to pull this off is to respond with another question and put the onus back on them.

These are my go-to responses:

- o What did you do to try and resolve the issue?
- o What's your solution to the problem?
- o So, what's the next step?
- o What do you think you should do?

Your message is the same regardless of the wording: If you're presenting me with a problem, you better have a solution before I weigh in. Responding with a question puts the ball back in their court and forces them to take ownership of both the problem and the solution.

If the dialog goes back and forth, end it with, "Let me know how it works out" to reiterate your expectation that the problem is to be solved by them. All of this, accompanied by follow up and feedback, will establish accountability as part of a healthy training environment.

When saying no isn't an option, you can always **pass the buck to somebody else**. There's nothing wrong with handing out a different business card or email address other than your own, so long as you offer a brief explanation. A straightforward statement like, "This is the best person to speak with" is fine, but I've always preferred injecting a little humor to ease the awkwardness. Handing a customer over to another sales associate because "they're smarter than you" or "they're the real expert" relays the same message without sounding rude.

If you value your time (and sanity), **see vendors and trade partners by appointment only.** Random drop-in visits are annoying, disruptive, and downright inefficient; they're just ill-prepared meetings with a one-sided agenda, or even worse, pointless check-ins to see how things are going.

There's a painless way to combat this without putting a strain on your relationship. When somebody drops in, apologize that you can't see them and request that they book a future appointment. Explain that this is a new policy you've implemented across the board and you appreciate their understanding.

This again circles back to training people to work within your schedule and not the other way around. Operate under a *no news is good news* policy, and inform them that if you need anything, you'll give them a call. Even the most stubborn or assertive individuals will come around after the second or third declined visit.

TIME-WIZARD TIP!

You can preemptively strike by emailing everyone about your new policy. Download this template at www.jeffhilderman.com/resources

Another way to protect your time is to subtly **say no to personal distractions and excessive communication**. The next time you're cornered by an employee who's rambling on about their chronic back pain, politely interrupt and request to hear the rest of the story later. You can evade ice-breaking small talk at the beginning of meetings, phone calls, and face-to-face conversations by getting right to the point and cueing others to do the same. When asked how you're doing, respond with, "Fine thanks, what can I do for you today?"

The right question asked with a positive and polite tone is all that's needed to prompt the other person to bench the small talk and get the real conversation going.

Minimizing redundant follow-ups is a similar strategy, where multiple inquiries can be eliminated with a single stroke. We live in a world of instant gratification, and people remain unsettled until they know you've read their email, touched their paperwork and made a decision. In these situations, the best defense is a good offense.

For instance, when given a catalog to review, tell the vendor that you'll have a look and be in touch before the end of the week. If the harassment begins anytime before then, politely shut it down with a straightforward response, such as "As per our previous conversation, I'll be in contact before the end of the week." There's no need to be rude, but you don't have to be warm and fuzzy either.

Whether it's a report, an email or anything else for that matter, anticipate the redundant follow-ups and cut them off at the pass. Reassure the person that their (enter important thing here) will be dealt with in a timely manner and stay true to your word.

MEETINGS: PREPARE TO DEFEND YOURSELF

The effectiveness of meetings has been scrutinized for years to either prove or debunk their actual benefit. There's no question that meetings can be long-winded, boring, and in some cases, even irrelevant, but I've found this has more to do with the people involved than the meeting itself. In a later chapter, I'll show you how to run an award-winning meeting, but for now, let's discuss ways to protect your time when you're in a bad one.

It's important to first determine which meetings you need to be a part of and which ones you don't. It's still a good idea to be actively involved in the weekly, monthly, and quarterly meetings with your management team, but beyond that, the value of your time should be carefully considered.

Ask yourself if the agenda requires your physical presence in the boardroom. Mid-level managers may request for you to sit in for many reasons, and while this may be necessary at first as part of the training process, it's not something they should grow accustomed to. In most cases, a copy of the meeting minutes is enough to stay informed.

If you're the control freak we talked about earlier, or love being in the spotlight, it's going to be equally important to protect your time from yourself. You can't afford to sit in on every committee meeting, and in fact, it can be more damaging if you do. Mid-level meetings are about your team, not you, and their ability to come together to formulate ideas and resolve issues. Even if you're quietly sitting in the corner, there will always be the temptation and expectation for you to intervene.

Think of it this way: You'd never invest your money into a stock that was guaranteed to yield a negative return on your investment, so how is this any different in the way you invest your time? Take a moment to consider all the meetings you could potentially remove yourself from, and let's talk about strategies that will enable you to do so.

The last thing you want to do is give others the impression that you're too important to be in the meeting, you're not a team player or that your time is more valuable than everybody else's. The most effective way I've found to navigate this minefield is to ask permission and substitute your time with something else deemed of equal or greater importance to them. In other words, sell them on why it's just as important that you're not in attendance, but present it as a choice. Your reasons will become theirs, and they'll convince themselves where your time is best spent.

Let's look at a few terrible ways to get out of a meeting along with their more suitable alternatives:

Terrible way	Replace with...
"Do I need to be there"	What's on the agenda? I can offer a few talking points ahead of time if you'd like, but I need to continue working on (blank). I hope you understand.
"I'm really busy"	I'm on a tight deadline to complete (blank), but I'd appreciate a copy of the minutes so I can review them afterward if that's ok.
"I have more important things to do"	I'm dealing with a time-sensitive matter at the moment, any chance I can sit this one out and get an update later?
"Go ahead without me"	Are you ok if I wasn't there for the meeting? You can update me with how everything went this afternoon.

Clearly communicating your objectives with transparency and relatable urgency will present a more sellable case for your absence, and greatly increase the odds of their approval. Just don't forget to follow through on any actionable items to bring yourself up to speed and reinforce your commitment to being a team player.

If there's no way to get out of a meeting, then follow this three-step strategy to keep things moving smoothly:

Step 1: No agenda? Request one!

How can you prepare for a meeting if you don't know what's being discussed? Similarly, if last minute meetings seem to be a reoccurring theme, respectfully request appropriate notice moving forward, so you have adequate time to prepare and schedule your day accordingly. Your concern is valid, and the solution is simple, so there shouldn't be any reason why it can't be accommodated.

Step 2: Stick to the agenda or bench it.

It's inevitable that meetings will branch off into sub-conversations, brainstorming sessions and debates, which is why establishing peer accountability is critical to keep everyone on topic. Even though the Chairperson is responsible for moderation, everyone should feel comfortable intervening when things get off track. All non-essential conversations, examples, stories and creative collaboration should be shut down or revisited if time prevails – yes, even for you.

Step 3: Stand up at the end of the meeting.

Stand up, to subtly cue that the conversation is over, and you'll be surprised how quickly everyone else follows suit. A hasty exit is the only chance you have to avoid getting dragged into the post-meeting small talk. This tactic is also highly effective in one-on-one meetings where the probability of getting trapped is even higher.

IN SUMMARY

If you're serious about reaching your goals, then you have to get serious about managing your time. We're all creatures of habit, but with the right systems in place to hold ourselves and others accountable, huge productivity gains can be achieved with minimal effort.

To keep ourselves in check, we must first understand where our time is best utilized and establish our rules of engagement. They can be internal protocols like responding to questions with another question, or external policies like *bring solutions, not problems.*

Likewise, rules of disengagement are useful to deflect incoming fire and navigate around sticky situations. Learning how to say no in different ways will help you evade unnecessary meetings, appointments, and conversations that don't pay a high return on your investment. Even when things are beyond your control, there's usually a way to minimize losses and leverage the situation to your advantage.

The success of this program relies on your ability to lead with ruthless efficiency, so take your time seriously, and others will do the same. In the next chapter, I'll show you how to get yourself organized so you can truly experience the power of efficiency.

Chapter 5

CLUTTERED DESK, CLUTTERED MIND

Albert Einstein famously remarked, "If a cluttered desk is the sign of a cluttered mind, of what then, is an empty desk a sign?" He was without question one of the most brilliant thinkers of our time, but I also get the impression that he was a little sensitive about his housekeeping habits.

We know chaos promotes creative thinking, but I would argue that this doesn't equate to disorganization. Artists and theorists may thrive in this environment while creating their content, but at some point, organization is still required to share their work and operate a business. This is even more paramount in the corporate world where growth and collaboration go hand in hand. So if your days are spent unraveling the mysteries of the universe, feel free to skip over this chapter, otherwise, let's begin to declutter your desk and your mind.

Think about how you manage your life, not just in terms of your time but on every level:

- o   What's your mindset when you arrive to work? Do you have a plan?
- o   Do you have a consistent daily routine or do you shoot from the hip?
- o   How do you deal with paperwork, calls, email, and appointments?
- o   How do you prepare for meetings?
- o   What's your approach to conflict resolution?
- o   How do you feel at the end of the day?
- o   What does your schedule look like tomorrow, a week or a month from now?

o   How do you balance your personal and professional obligations while still making time for yourself?

o   How do you keep all the moving parts running together smoothly?

All of us need organization in our lives – literally. Our brains are hardwired to process information in a systematic order so that we can prioritize activities and make informed decisions. Even when we're fast asleep, our brains are hard at work organizing our thoughts, feelings, and experiences into different compartments.

Organization is the common denominator between leadership, communication, time management, and productivity, influencing the success we'll see in both our personal and professional lives. Whether you're the CEO of your company or your family, getting everything accomplished requires a plan and the organizational skills to make it happen.

THE PI FILING SYSTEM

The first step is to adopt the correct filing system so you can maintain order around your desk. I'd like to emphasize *correct* because throwing everything in a pile doesn't count. **The Priority-Importance (PI) Filing System** is an effortless method to organize your paperwork and prioritize tasks.

Priority	Importance	Done By	When
High	High	You	Now
High	Low	Somebody Else	Now
Low	High	You	Later
Low	Low	Nobody	Never

You'll need three vertically-stacked trays on your desk, the top being your general inbox for all incoming paperwork. As it's sorted, all High-High items remain in the top tray so they can be dealt with immediately following the sorting process. Urgent items which can be delegated to others are given a High-Low rank and placed in the second tray. The bottom tray is reserved for Low-High items, which are still important enough to be dealt with by you, but at a more convenient time.

As for Low-Low items, this is the true clutter we have a tendency to hoard, and so we must apply the *Three-Month Rule* to determine its value: If the document will likely be used in the next three months, file it away in another location. If not, throw it away without overthinking it. If it's important enough, it will likely re-emerge in your inbox, and you'll have another opportunity to reconsider its fate.

It's easy to work the PI Filing System into your daily routine. When you first start out, review the various types of paperwork you deal with on a regular basis and assign a PI rank to each. After a week, you'll have a better feel for the process and be able to file your paperwork at a glance. Your inbox only needs to be checked once or twice a day, but **the golden rule is that the top two trays must be empty before you go home (on time).**

BONUS TIP!

Create an action area on your desk where all the actual *work* happens and restrict this zone to only one item at a time. Each piece of paper should only be handled twice: once to organize, and again to deal with it.

As you work through this book, take notice of how much paperwork is transferred from the top tray to the middle. This is a good indication of your willingness to let go of your work, and it serves as a progress benchmark. Once you get into the groove, your pile should continue to decrease in size until you have three empty trays on your desk – and that's an extremely satisfying feeling.

INBOX ZERO

Let's now turn our attention to your inbox and start cleaning house! The sight of unread messages in the hundreds or even thousands is enough to give anyone a jolt. With a few useful tools, you can make your email work for you instead of the other way around.

A good rule of thumb is that you should have no more than three email accounts at any given time: one for work, another for personal use, and a third for trash, which I'll explain in a moment. Some people might disagree with me, but I prefer using a single account for both work and personal use to keep everything in one place. My email is organized with specific folders and labels so I can quickly find anything with a few clicks. This is a standard feature for Gmail and virtually every other provider out there.

I'd recommend creating a main folder for personal email and another for work email, including subfolders in each one for further organization, such as *Bills* or *Family*. Color-coated labels (or flags) can also be used to prioritize your emails, meaning you can apply the PI Filing System we discussed earlier to your messages as well.

Alternatively, you can set up filters within your email settings to automate this process and have the high priority items bumped to the top of your unread list if you'd like. There are plenty of tutorials on the web that can show you how to do this, and I strongly encourage you to check them out if you're unsure what to do.

There's another cool function in Gmail's settings called *Send and Archive*, which automatically transfers any replied email threads from your inbox to a separate archived folder. This hidden gem is an often overlooked feature that can declutter your inbox from conversations which have come and gone. Even as you're reading this now, I would assume there are new tools available to improve the quality of your life, so do a little digging to see what else you can find.

As for the endless supply of junk mail you can't seem to escape, I have a solution for that as well. If you can't resist the urge to sign up for a contest or survey, be sure to use the trash email account I mentioned earlier. This bogus account funnels the majority of spam into a single place and far from everything else that's of actual value.

When junk mail finds its way into your real inbox, deal with it immediately! By law, there must be an unsubscribe button somewhere (usually at the bottom), and it takes less than ten seconds to do so. If the amount of email to unsubscribe from is overwhelming, there are third-party apps worth looking into, such as *Unroll.Me* (free) that can identify, tally, and delete unwanted subscriptions with a single click.

GO ONE STEP FURTHER

Your computer is an extension of your workspace, so keeping that desktop clean is just as important as the top of your actual desk. Having more than a dozen key folders on your desktop is just asking for trouble, and if you need a dumping ground, create a folder for such a purpose.

It's highly inefficient to scour your monitor every time you need to locate a file, especially considering how often this happens in a day. If you can't manage this yourself, consider using your operating system's desktop clean-up tool, or spend a few bucks on a third-party app to get the job done.

DECLUTTER YOUR BRAIN

While a cluttered space can inhibit productivity, a cluttered mind can be worse in many ways. It can lead to impaired focus, judgment and memory problems, anxiety and exhaustion, all of which can take a serious toll on your health – and your bottom line. So what's the prescription for an oversaturated brain? Just a pen and paper.

At the end of each day, purge your thoughts by writing everything you can think of down on paper. Avoid the sticky notes and instead opt for a notebook or even better, a daily organizer with dates, page numbers, and calendars to maintain a permanent record of your thoughts. Your ideas, opinions, concerns, and checklists need to be kept somewhere, so better in a book than inside your head. This is how I learned to decompress before coming home so I could be present with my family on my personal time.

So there you have it: a few solid strategies to manage what's on your desk, on your computer, and in your head. In the next chapter, we'll pull everything together to reinvent your daily routine and setup the necessary fail-safes to keep both you and your team focused on the right things.

Chapter 6

YOUR DAILY ROUTINE

I firmly believe that the majority of my success, both at work and at home, is attributed to my daily routine. I wake up every morning at 6:00 am and begin the day with *me* time. While everyone else is asleep, I'm able to write, exercise or do anything else I want without negotiation or compromise. It's one of my favorite parts of the day and my motivation for going to bed early.

I'm also a list guy, and get immense satisfaction from putting a check in a box. I know it's quirk of mine and that it sometimes drives other people nuts, but it's also one of the main reasons why I'm a super productive person. Whether it's cutting the grass or taking my kids to the park, I like to put things on a list and knock them off one by one.

The same holds true for my work. I always have a plan before I walk through the door and know exactly what I want to accomplish each day. My first hour is dedicated to touching base with my team, communicating new objectives and ensuring old ones are completed to my satisfaction. After I've set everyone up for the day, I can comfortably head to my office and work on my own projects knowing that everyone else is on track and working on the right things.

I also have a special routine every night when I come home. I make time to play with my kids, chase them around the house and tickle them before bed. We read stories, say our goodnights, and of course, fill up the glass of water a second time. My wife and I spend most nights with our feet up, watching our favorite shows in our pajamas. It's the perfect end to a busy day!

This may sound too good to be true, but I can assure you it's entirely within your reach. I'd also like to point out that structure doesn't equate to rigidity. My day is still flexible enough to account for spontaneity, but structure is what keeps me focused on my priorities.

I wish I could tell you that there's a secret formula for striking the perfect work-life balance, but the truth is it really just comes down to two things: structure and discipline. Developing the right daily routine will ensure everything important at work gets done on time, so you're free to live life when you're off the clock.

SIXTY-SIX DAYS

Don't be fooled by marketing campaigns promising life-altering change in thirty days, because statistically speaking, it's not going to happen. A recent study[1] published in the *European Journal of Social Psychology* showed that on average, it takes more than twice this time to form positive habits, sixty-six days to be exact, and within this period, we are most susceptible to failure.

To keep the odds in your favor, you'll need a routine that's both rigid (to promote consistency) and flexible (to account for the daily unknowns). In other words, a system that can be easily integrated into your life and will continue to work for you until the right habits are formed.

Your daily routine is where the rubber meets the road, aligning your actions with your personal beliefs. It's the difference between knowing what to do and doing it consistently without hesitation.

A one-size fits all approach won't work for everyone, but consider the following guidelines as a place to start:

○ Wake up early, and with a sense of purpose

○ Orientate yourself with the day's events

○ Motivate your team and provide clear direction

---

[1] Lally, P., van Jaarsveld, C. H. M., Potts, H. W. W. and Wardle, J. (2010), How are habits formed: Modelling habit formation in the real world. Eur. J. Soc. Psychol., 40: 998-1009. doi:10.1002/ejsp.674.

- o Consolidate and prioritize your personal tasks

- o Schedule your breaks

- o Follow up and reenergize your team

- o Brain purge and plan for tomorrow

YOUR MORNING RITUAL

It's no coincidence that the go-getters of the world are more successful than everybody else. They are driven by productivity, not comfort, and are willing to sacrifice more in the short-term knowing that there's a bigger payout down the road.

Successful leaders wake up one to three hours earlier than everybody else because they understand the personal benefit and tactical advantage it gives them over their competition. This block of time is reserved for anything requiring deep concentration, as it's the only guaranteed distraction-free period of their day. It's the perfect opportunity to work on creative projects, troubleshoot problems, or schedule upcoming events.

If you'd rather hit the gym, meditate, or simply enjoy a cup of coffee while reading the newspaper, that's ok too! The intent is to establish your own morning ritual and prime your brain before heading off to work. You don't have to be a morning person to get up early, you just have to be willing to go to bed earlier the night before.

STEPPING INTO THE RING

Mike Tyson said it best: "Everybody has a plan until they get punched in the face." This is what usually happens shortly after we arrive at work. We have a plan, things go sideways, and we have to adapt to the situation. It's part of life, and there's no way to avoid it, but you can certainly soften the blow.

Knowing what to expect will help you prepare for the fight, but situational awareness inside the ring will determine if you take one on the chin or get your lights knocked out. Likewise, your top priority when you get to work is to familiarize yourself with who's there, what's happening and how will your plans be executed. If you don't know what's going on, your plan is useless, and you'll quickly lose control of your day.

FACE TIME

It's your primary responsibility as the leader to guide and motivate your team first thing in the morning. It's all too easy to retreat to your hideaway and dive into your own work, but if you don't clarify company goals, outline your expectations and set the pace for the day, who will?

But you also need to be thinking a bigger game.

Your employees *need* direction, but what they really *want* is your attention. They want to be noticed, applauded for their contributions and to feel valued, only then will they truly produce their best work. **The secret to getting the most out of your team is to satisfy their social needs and take an interest in their personal lives.** Luckily, all of this can be accomplished with a little face time each morning.

BONUS TIP!

Accompany your morning greeting with a personalized message or question. You can inquire about their weekend or ask how their daughter's recital went. The personal touch will humanize your "boss" image and show your employees that you care.

The added benefit of these mini conversations is that they naturally open the door to any questions your employees may have. In reality, they'll find you in your office anyway, so you're better to get all of the distractions out of the way as soon as possible. Some conversations will occupy more time than others but remember, it's a way to resolve issues early on and demonstrate your willingness to support the team.

FULL STEAM AHEAD

Now that your employees are on cruise control, you can finally tackle your own work. In order to prioritize tasks and maximize your productivity, take a moment to reflect on the following:

- o   When is my power hour, the time when my mind is the sharpest?
- o   Which tasks can I consolidate and do only once or twice a day?
- o   When do I need a break to recharge my mind and body?

It doesn't matter when your peak performance is, so long as you're using it to work on the big-ticket items. These are usually the low priority, high importance tasks which get pushed back due to insufficient time or focus. Remember that walls are built one brick at a time, so dedicate your power hour to laying those bricks, and eventually, your project will take shape.

If you want to boost your efficiency, begin by ditching the multitasking philosophy. People love to throw this term around because they associate it with increased productivity and efficiency, when in fact, this couldn't be farther from the truth. We only have 100% of our attention as a whole, and every time we introduce another task, we divide our time and focus accordingly. In our mind, we think we're getting three or four things done simultaneously, but really, we're just doing crappy work across the board.

For every instance we're distracted, it can take up to thirty minutes to get our brain back to where it was. So do the math on a handful of distractions as a result of multitasking, and it's no wonder why we can't get anything accomplished.

You'll see some of your biggest time gains when you consolidate redundant tasks, such as returning phone calls, answering emails, and processing paperwork. All of this is important, but generally low in priority in the sense that it can be lumped together and dealt with once or twice a day.

In my personal experience, I've discovered that the best time to put myself in airplane mode and catch up on this work is directly after lunch. It's late enough in the day to catch the majority of inbound paperwork and messages, but early enough to respond to anything urgent. I close my door, silence my phone, and can usually plow through everything in about an hour.

There's nothing wrong with being unavailable for an hour or two each day, and frankly, it sends the proper message to your team to respect your time and consolidate their own inquiries. Employees always have reasons to distract you, so it's important to communicate when there's an open-door policy and when there isn't.

SLOW DOWN TO SPEED UP

You're not a robot so stop acting like one. It doesn't matter what's going on or how busy you are, breaks are an absolute must. Stepping away from your work for even ten minutes can help you reframe your thoughts, reduce stress, and capture a second wind. Physically schedule it into your day planner and hold yourself accountable.

By taking a break, I mean it in the most literal sense – having a coffee and talking about work doesn't count. Go for a walk outside, listen to music, read a book, or do anything else that mentally removes you from your work environment. If you have an office, close the door and break out the yoga mat – your body and your brain will love you for it.

ROUND TWO

Around mid-afternoon, either before or after airplane mode, is another good time to check in with the troops. You lit the fuse first thing in the morning, now's the time to follow up on their work and offer encouragement.

If the job was completed on time and to your expectations, commend them in public and get them going on something else. If not, take corrective action as required and inject them with a second dose of motivation. When your team expects you to follow up on their assigned duties, they will work hard for your praise and at your pace, rather than their own.

BRAIN PURGE

We already discussed the importance of clearing your head and how daily planning begins the night before. Block out the final twenty minutes of your day to mentally tie up loose ends and formulate a game plan for tomorrow. Jot down your questions and concerns, the people you need to speak with, and the things requiring additional follow-up. Like everything else we've covered in this chapter, be sure to schedule it every day until it becomes habitual.

This officially concludes our conversation on time management, and you're more than ready to put everything into practice right now! Don't wait, because the more time you can free up now, the easier it will be to implement the rest of this book.

The final chapters in this section are dedicated to the fundamental elements of leadership. I want you to become the absolute best leader you can be going into this program, so your clone is the best version of you. Buckle up, because your crash course on leadership begins right now.

.

Chapter 7

BOSS OR LEADER?

Being *the leader* and being *a leader* are two very different things. For instance, it's possible for someone to acquire great power by circumstance without displaying the attributes of a leader; similarly, someone with virtually no authority whatsoever can rise to become an extraordinary leader. It's easy to confuse the two because we often use the term leader interchangeably to distinguish rank and responsibility. But true leadership as a verb, meaning to lead, is something you do, not something you are.

Anyone can be the leader if they are placed into a position of power. It's their responsibility to monitor procedures, enforce policies, and drive results. There's no long-term vision or strategic plan – their priority is to maintain the status quo and keep things running as efficiently as possible.

A boss influences behavior through manipulation, knowing how to play on the emotions of others to get what they want, when they want it. They may be charismatic, generous with incentives or blatantly use scare tactics to bend others to their will. Their employees follow direction out of necessity rather than loyalty and work just hard enough to stay under the radar and collect a paycheck.

On the other hand, a true leader only needs two things: a purpose and a following. They see themselves as instruments to communicate their vision and unite others who share similar beliefs. They influence behavior by pointing to a destination and giving a reason to charge forward. Leadership is about forging relationships and inseparable bonds, where the group follows the leader through thick and thin not because they have to, but because they're inspired to.

A Boss...	A Leader...
Is chosen by the company	Is chosen by the people
Has a Mission	Has a Vision
Persuades Action	Inspires Action
Upholds Policies	Upholds Values
Leads By Authority	Leads by Example
Drives Results	Fosters Team Spirit
Promotes Fear	Promotes Trust
Listens to Respond	Listens to Understand
Communicates Down	Communicates Across

ANYONE CAN BE A LEADER

I learned this lesson when I was fourteen, working for a fast food franchise. It was my first real job, and I had absolutely no experience. The training was terrible, the managers were arrogant, and needless to say, camaraderie wasn't in their vocabulary. I wanted to quit after a month, but my parents insisted I stick it out.

I decided if I wasn't going anywhere, then I might as well make the best of my situation. I took the initiative to teach myself how to do the job properly and put forth my best effort. Whenever I observed somebody else struggling with a similar task, I'd step in and offer assistance where I could. Before long, I had all sorts of people asking me for help in areas beyond my expertise, but at least half the time we were able to figure it out together. Ironically, even my managers solicited my advice for things I had assumed they had the answers to.

Even though I held no official title, people looked to me for guidance. I couldn't figure out why because after all, there were people hired to fill this role. But what I determined years later, is that **leadership is in the eye of the beholder.**

I wanted to see my colleagues succeed. I listened, asked questions, and solved other people's problems despite receiving little training myself. I tried to make everyone's job a little easier, they took notice and appreciated it.

Two years later, I accepted a supervisory position, oversaw a team of twenty people, and hit the jackpot with a fifty-cent raise. But my official promotion didn't really change anything because, in the eyes of my co-workers, I had already been elected their leader a year earlier.

LEADERS EVERYWHERE

Leadership is a mentality and a specific way of doing things. It's not bound by rank or responsibility, and therefore it's possible to have leaders at any level within an organization. Consider the typical pyramid hierarchy where the President or General Manager is at the top calling the shots. Below this person is usually some level of mid-management, comprised of individuals who employ limited authority to govern their respective teams.

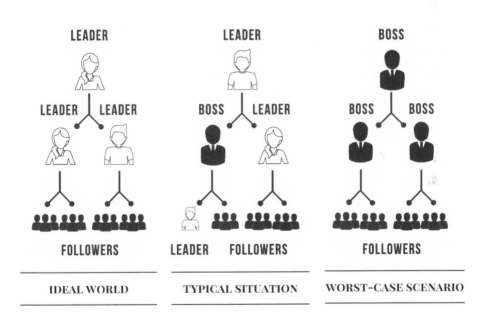

In an ideal world, every person in a position of authority exhibits the qualities of a leader and the organization as a whole presents a united front. But as you know this is rarely the case.

In the second scenario, the Leader is still leading and has a clear sense of direction, but mid-level management lacks the necessary knowledge or skills to lead in a similar capacity. This is where most businesses usually end up and where the real need for your clone comes into play.

Every now and then, companies may be lucky enough to find an employee who just *gets it*. Even if they're working underneath a boss and hold no official position of authority, these individuals, who naturally possess the attributes of a leader, will instinctively pick up the slack and assist in leading the team. These are your A-Team players who should be personally coached by the Leader and groomed for a future management role.

The third and worst-case scenario is when the organization is deprived of leadership at all levels. The Leader may be the highest-ranking officer, but unfortunately, that's where it ends. They have either neglected to establish the company's vision and values, failed to inspire their team, or have not personally walked the talk themselves to promote buy-in. Any organization without a minimum level of leadership is in big trouble and prone to a self-destructive culture.

THE VERDICT

So are you a boss or a leader? If you're still unsure, look no further than your team:

- o Do they demonstrate an eager-to-please attitude?

- o Are they company-minded and excited to share new ideas?

- o Do they jump on board with your new ideas?

- o Are they honest and transparent with you?

- o Can they tell you why the company exists and the role they serve?

The Million Dollar Question

If you shut down your business and started a new venture, would your team follow you?

Now that you understand the differences between a boss and a leader, you may be surprised to find that not all leaders are created equal, nor are they all successful. In the next chapter, I'll show you exactly what it takes to come out on top, regardless of what's thrown your way.

Chapter 8

EFFECTIVE LEADERSHIP

Leaders inspire others to take action, but inspiration alone doesn't guarantee the vision will be fulfilled. Imagine you're an architect and have just designed a beautiful building. You've convinced investors to put up the money and the various trades to commit to the project. Everybody's on board, but now what?

- o Who's in charge and how are problems to be addressed?
- o Has everyone seen the blueprints and are they on the same page?
- o What are your timelines, budgets, and other constraints?
- o Can you say for certain that everyone has the full scope of your vision?

You may have inspired everyone to sign up, but this doesn't mean they fully understand what to do and what's expected of them. Even under the most optimistic circumstances where everyone could work together without explicit instruction, chances are, it's not going to turn out exactly as hoped.

Then we have **effective leadership,** which is the act of guiding the inspired to fulfill the vision. It's the physical execution of the plan, ensuring tasks are understood, supervised, and accomplished. The difference between leadership and effective leadership is the latter takes the needs of both the leader and the followers into consideration. The leader, as we know, needs a purpose and a following. But what about the followers, what do they need?

Like the leader, **followers also need a purpose**. There must be an aspiration for change, otherwise, what's the point? This could be a problem in need of a solution, a new challenge or an opportunity to grow for the sake of progression.

Secondly, **followers need to be inspired**. They must be presented with an alternative scenario with a positive outcome, one which instills hope amidst doubt, and courage in the presence of fear. Followers have all sorts of excuses to not take action, but inspiration puts the spotlight on the single, most important reason why they should.

Finally, **followers need direction**; a clear path from where they stand to the final destination. Without direction, followers may be reluctant to blindly follow the leader on a whim, and they may bring everything to a halt before it even begins. Likewise, if they're unsure what to do or the role they'll play, their actions could be misaligned with the leader's vision.

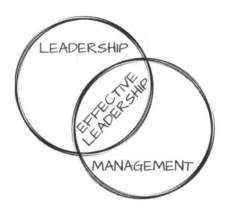

Walt Disney was one of the greatest visionaries of his time, and his attention to detail was second to none. His perfectionism extended into every aspect of his company, and over a half century later remains deeply engrained in the Disney culture we know today. When Walt inspired all the necessary people to build Disneyland, he didn't sit back and watch other people build it. He was on site, consistently monitoring the details until everyone got it right.

Direction isn't just about communicating the plan. Effective leaders are extremely protective of their vision and keep an eye on the finer details without getting lost in the logistics of how. When they observe something that isn't right, it's addressed and corrected on the spot. Walt lived what he believed and proved dreams really do come true, but only after putting in the necessary work to bring that vision to life.

> **Effective Leadership =**Purpose x Inspiration x Direction

This is the magic formula for accomplishing great things, even when monumental challenges are present. It's the combination of purpose, inspiration, and direction which will allow you to build a passionate army, break down barriers, and consistently outperform the competition. Effective leaders are the ones who set out to do the impossible and make it viable for the rest of us.

QUALITIES OF AN EFFECTIVE LEADER

There are great leaders everywhere, in every industry and type of organization. They have different leadership styles, beliefs, areas of expertise, and certainly different visions. But despite these vast differences, effective leaders share certain qualities enabling them to bring their vision to fruition and inspire others to do the same.

Passion is the ultimate competitive advantage. Leaders who focus on things they deeply care about are more likely to excel in their role because they naturally tap into their own beliefs, interests, and talents. Their work is rewarding instead of a chore, and they're willing to make the necessary sacrifices because they believe it's the right thing to do. Passionate leaders lead with authenticity, and when their message feels real, others step in line to follow.

Perception is the art of observation and interpretation. Effective leaders rely on their situational awareness to stay ahead of the curve. They observe mannerisms, notice details, ask questions and absorb information like a sponge. They're also sensitive to people's emotions and quickly adapt their own behavior to suit their circumstances. Leaders are expected to do the right thing, but doing so requires them to intuitively assess each situation and draw from past experiences to make the appropriate decision.

Empathy is the understanding and appreciation of people's feelings; the ability to put yourself in somebody else's shoes and consider how your actions will impact them. It's the human element of leadership that promotes a feeling of safety within the group, knowing their leader has their best interests at heart. Effective leaders listen intently, take unbiased perspectives and make decisions based on a win-win approach. Empathy forges trust and opens the lines of communication so information can flow freely in both directions.

It's important for leaders to keep themselves in check, using **self-awareness** to recognize and regulate their emotions. They understand how their feelings affect their ability to think, communicate, and make decisions, all of which influence the overall performance of their team.

Leaders lacking self-awareness are unable to gage the emotional needs of others and have difficulty relating to them on a personal level. When emotional reactions are left unfiltered, they can jeopardize relationships and potentially damage the company's vision and culture.

Team-building is a prerequisite for leadership, but this goes beyond mobilizing its members to take action. It's a never-ending cycle of performance assessment, alignment, and feedback to develop individual strengths and group proficiency.

Effective leaders are mentors who openly share knowledge and personal experiences so others can learn from their mistakes. They foster a supportive environment where differences are embraced, knowing the additional skills and perspectives will only improve the team's capabilities. Effective leaders see the potential in everyone and are committed to personal development.

The path from A to B isn't always clear: plans fall apart, new challenges appear out of thin air, and occasionally, team morale takes a hit. But leaders who demonstrate **perseverance** don't allow themselves to get discouraged. They're used to being outside of their comfort zone and are committed to making the idea work – regardless of what everyone else thinks. Effective leaders take control of their own destiny and see their vision through to the end come hell or high water.

EFFECTIVE LEADERSHIP STYLES

Success doesn't come from a single style of leadership, but rather the ability to work within a spectrum and choose the appropriate style for the situation. Not surprisingly, leaders default to whatever style they're most comfortable with, given their personality, values, and experience. There are three styles of leadership on the **Passive-Assertive (PA) Spectrum**, each with its own set of advantages and drawbacks.

It's important for leaders to know where they naturally fall on this spectrum so they can recognize how their actions influence their team and determine which approach is best suited for the situation at hand.

The Captain: "This is how we do it."

Benefits:

- o   Provides clear and concise direction
- o   Sets the pace to obtain the quickest results
- o   Minimizes the probability and severity of mistakes

Use When:

- o   Goals are detail-oriented or time-sensitive
- o   Introducing new concepts during training
- o   Team is highly competent and self-motivated

Potential Problems:

- Doesn't empower others to make decisions or take the initiative
- Lacks creative input from others
- Conversation is limited to tasks and objectives
- Doesn't build relationships or develop skills
- Extended use can lead to employee burnout

The Collaborator: "Let's discuss how to do it."

Benefits:

- Breaks vision down into bite-sized segments
- Promotes participation and the flow of creative ideas, perspectives and feedback
- Everyone can contribute to the vision using their own strengths
- Creates camaraderie within the group
- Individuals feel valued and fulfilled

Use When:

- Brainstorming new ideas and solutions
- Team morale is weak
- Establishing peer accountability
- The leader wants to step back and let the group facilitate logistics of the vision

Potential Problems:

- Not every idea is a winner, leading to hurt feelings and resentment
- Group can miss their mark and require the leader's intervention
- Extended use can lead to analysis paralysis

The Coach: "How do you want to do it?"

Benefits:

- o Focus placed on goal-setting and personal development
- o Improves rapport between the leader and the individuals within the group
- o Creates a safe environment to build trust and self-confidence
- o Individual attention boosts morale

Use When:

- o Developing values and skills for long-term success
- o The leader is open-minded to approach their vision in different ways
- o Providing constructive feedback to deal with sensitive issues
- o There are inconsistent levels of proficiency within the group

Potential Problems:

- o May take longer to produce results based on the experience of team
- o Extended use can divert leader's attention from the big picture

 DON'T WORRY!
No specific style is better or worse than the other. In fact, your default position may change over time based on your vision or the challenges and capabilities of your team.

So where do you find yourself on the PA Spectrum? If you're still unsure of what your dominant style is, refer back to the daily activities you logged in your journal. The manner in which you engaged your team, solved problems, and directed traffic will emulate one style over the others. Remember, leaders who are perceptive and self-aware can feel out what's working and what's not, and when necessary, switch gears to get the results they're looking for.

As for me, I've spent the majority of my career somewhere between collaborator and captain. I've always had a dominant personality, and despite my passion for developing others, I have a tendency to do whatever it takes to protect my vision.

That said, I've spent the last five years as a coach more than the other two styles. This is in part because my priorities have changed as I've matured as a leader, and also because I now have an army of clones (also known as my management team) who already understand my vision and expectations.

* * *

We covered a lot of ground in this section, and it's my hope that you've found a few tips along the way which will help polish your skills as a leader. After all, the more time invested in the original you, the more refined your clone will be.

Let's move on to Section Two, where we'll officially kick off the first thirty days of the cloning program. Most people will find this part to be the most intense, so take notes as you go and don't speed through. If you have a physical copy of this book, I'd recommend taking a highlighter to it so you can quickly refer back to the parts that resonate with you.

When you're ready, let's dive in.

Section Two

DRAFTING YOUR BLUEPRINT

Chapter 9

THE BIG PICTURE

Ask any entrepreneur what they do, and they'll default to a scripted response. Ask how they do it, and they'll talk for hours if you let them. But ask *why* they do it, and they'll likely be at a loss for words. If you don't believe me, try it for yourself. It's not as easy as it sounds, and this is why so many entrepreneurs get stuck in their business.

Explaining the *whats* and *hows* are effortless because this is how we naturally interact with one another. Our communication tends to scratch the surface and provide just enough information so the other person gets it, and then we move on to the next topic. We aren't used to getting into deep conversation, or deep thought for that matter, and when we do, the clarity of our message often takes a nose dive.

The underlying problem for many entrepreneurs is that **they either don't fully understand the big picture themselves, or they struggle to articulate it and get others on board.** Consequently, this creates a disconnect between communication and comprehension, resulting in decreased productivity, costly mistakes, and a demoralized workforce.

When it comes to conveying the big picture, close enough isn't good enough. It's your responsibility as the sole proprietor of your vision to create the blueprint, set goals, and outline expectations. Only then, can this information be effectively used to provide direction and hold others accountable for their actions.

Up to this point, you've survived on intuition, experience, and sheer guts, but don't expect your clone to be so lucky. A true clone represents you inside and out, meaning you'll first need to put in the work to figure out exactly who you are, what you believe, and where you want to be.

Like I said, the first thirty days are tough. Self-reflection plays a significant role during this process, and it can be challenging to get everything out of your head and onto paper– especially if transcribing isn't your forte. But don't sweat it, there will be plenty of time for revision. The most important thing right now is to be as thoughtful and thorough as you can.

Chapter 10

LET'S TALK CULTURE

Every business is unique in its own way. From internal practices to public relations, there's a specific way of doing things known as organizational culture. It stems from the leader's vision and values; over time, becoming the shared belief system of the entire group.

Culture also represents the organization's health in terms of team morale, engagement, and cohesiveness. It's the sense of collective responsibility and willingness to help one another succeed and put the group's needs before individual self-interests.

Culture exists in every organization, good or bad, and is the deal maker or breaker for most people. So, what does an unhealthy organizational culture look like? From within, it's a pretty inhospitable place: pettiness, selfishness, tension, hostility, dishonesty, greed, the list goes on and on. Leaders command respect but lack integrity, while employees gossip, argue, blame, and do the absolute minimum to get by. In this environment, everyone has a breaking point, and even the most loyal and well-compensated employees will decide that the misery just isn't worth it. They move on, their replacements go through the meat-grinder, and sadly, this becomes the norm.

For anyone lucky enough to have dodged this bullet first hand, I'm sure you've still experienced the fallout as a consumer. The place is a dump, the service is terrible, and nobody seems too concerned about negative feedback. When employees suffer, the company's efficiency and reputation suffer as well. It's quite possible for a business to be profitable in the short-term with an unhealthy culture, but just like its employees, customers are only willing to endure so much before something has to give.

By contrast, a healthy organizational culture is pure magic. For starters, it attracts the best talent who are passionate about their work and driven to help others. Whatever they lack in credentials is made up ten-fold with their positive demeanor and can-do attitude. They're the self-motivators you've been looking for to champion your cause and become ambassadors of your vision.

Having the best people on your team will not only continue to attract more of the same but will also attract the best type of customer to your business. Customers who are willing to pay more for the additional value you provide – whether it's higher quality, convenience or simply a more enjoyable experience. **That's right, your customers don't care about price, they care about value.** And when you bring something special to the table, people go crazy for it! Obviously, this is great for sales, but it also raises the bar for your competition.

Your customers are human beings and naturally attracted to what's new and exciting in the marketplace. Even though they love you, they can't help but occasionally pop over to the competition to see if the grass is greener on the other side of the fence. The secret to bringing them back is to raise their expectations so high that they're left utterly disappointed everywhere else they go. With the right culture, you can accomplish the seemingly impossible and set a pace your competition struggles to keep up with.

One of your clone's most important duties is to preserve the organization's culture exactly as you would – the key word being *preserve*. As the leader, it's your responsibility to first define what the organization must be (even if it's not there right now), so everyone clearly understands what's expected of them.

DEVELOPING CULTURE

Thus far we've treated culture as a single entity, but in reality, this is not the case. In the beginning, when the founder is at the helm and working with a handful of employees, culture can be defined and managed with relative ease. But as the business grows in size and complexity, so do the challenges of maintaining a single culture everyone identifies with. Consequently, two types of culture begin to emerge – global and local.

Global culture is the primary culture spread across the entire organization, where the leader's belief system is universally accepted by the group. But as employees begin to branch off into subsidiary bodies based on department, position, and proximity (to name a few), a secondary or **local culture** takes shape. This culture represents a closer family dynamic, where there's wiggle room for individual personalities and values. And just as cultures differ from business to business, so do the local cultures under the same roof.

For example, let's say that a manufacturing plant has a healthy organizational culture and all of its employees have adopted its vision and values as their own. Now consider the various departments within the company such as administration, assembly, sales, shipping, and receiving.

Given the different leadership styles within each department, along with the respective personalities of the team, it's entirely possible that multiple local cultures could exist. The sales team could be a tight-knit social group that enjoys a little friendly competition, while everyone in administration quietly keeps to themselves. Both are acceptable, so long as the groups can work harmoniously to complete their objectives.

Don't forget about the most important aspect of all – customers! The attitudes of the company are best reflected by the manner in which they serve. Nothing is private behind closed doors, and the customer experience is the ultimate tell-all sign of who cares and who doesn't. Therefore, we must consider both the internal and external elements of culture, similar to the relationship between action and consequence.

So to recap, we know that global and local cultures coexist within the business. We also know the company's inward beliefs are channeled outward to form the customer experience. As a result, the combination of these two principles produces the four variables of organizational culture.

Outward Global is the set of standardized behaviors carried out by the group, representing the company's **Mission**. The team's collective actions are experienced and observed by the outside world, forming what will eventually become the company's brand.

Inward Global unifies everyone within the organization under a single belief system, known as the company's **Core Values**. These values translate to the organization's code of conduct, ultimately governing the decisions and actions of the group.

Inward Local is an agreed way of doing things unique to a particular group within the organization. These **Performance Standards** are the non-negotiable criteria outlined by the leader to promote consistency and quality throughout the team.

Outward Local is where the physical actions of an employee take place. **Service Guidelines** are used as performance recommendations to enhance the customer experience and increase efficiency while granting individual liberties best suited to their personality.

Everything the organization says, believes, and does revolves around the leader's vision. **The Cultural Framework** is the transcript of this vision and the playbook for how it will be fulfilled by the group. When defined, this framework will also serve as the company's foundation and support all future endeavors.

IMPLEMENTING THE RIGHT CULTURE

Depending on the status of your own company's culture, the work involved may range from minor tweaks to a complete overhaul. Every business has obstacles to overcome, but with the right plan and firm hand on their shoulder, employees can make the transition with minimal bumps and bruises.

There are **three fundamental changes** that must occur before an employee will adapt to a new culture. They must:

1. Change what is known, by <u>understanding</u> the new way of doing things

2. Change what is believed, by <u>observing</u> others model the behavior

3. Change what is habitual, by consistently <u>doing</u> the right things

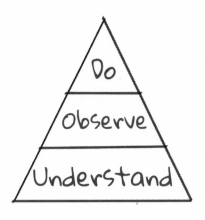

Understand

Knowledge has the power to sway decisions and influence behavior, but the key to unlocking it hinges on effective communication. Tread lightly here, because I see leaders mess this up all the time and blow up their entire plan before it even gets off the ground. They take abrupt corrective measures without warning or explanation, consequently rubbing their employees the wrong way and exasperating the problem.

The leader's rash decisions to override employees, change policies, restructure teams and take disciplinary action are a disservice to the organization and jeopardize the integrity of their personal brand. Employees can't change what they don't understand, and they will never buy into the new culture so long as they're left in the dark and treated as the problem instead of the solution.

This again circles back to the fundamental question of why. Why is the company's trajectory off course and why does it matter? The transparency will clear the air and funnel employees toward compliance, whereas gaps in the story will most certainly lead to speculation, gossip, and confusion.

When your team understands why the change is necessary, the subsequent *what* and *how* are finally brought into context. In order to effectively convey this message, you'll need to carefully consider your content and delivery system. What you say is important, but how you say it will dictate the level of their comprehension and retention.

Your content is based on the Cultural Framework we just discussed and can be reworked into a variety of training materials such as handbooks, job descriptions, and evaluations. It's crucial to formalize all of this in writing because it will:

- ✓ Legitimize *the new way* of doing things
- ✓ Clarify expectations and individual responsibilities
- ✓ Promote consistency throughout the entire organization

This is where the significance of your delivery system comes into play. Documenting your content is important, but without proper execution, your message will fall on deaf ears. Teams are crippled by the corporate mentality of creating wordy, overly complex manuals that say everything and nothing at the same time. Don't assume that posting a vision statement on the wall or throwing a manual in front of an employee is going to generate buy-in because it won't.

Consider which has a greater impact on your future behavior: receiving a speeding ticket in the mail or nervously handing over your license and registration to a police officer? Are you more likely to feel appreciated with a thank you note, or with the squeeze of a loving hug? The point is that communication becomes highly effective when it's delivered with a personal touch and leaves a lasting impression on the other person.

Applying the same philosophy to your delivery systems will enable you to make emotional connections with your team and inspire them to take action. Consider giving a live presentation to your employees to get them on board, and field any questions or concerns they may have. Additionally, you could work a similar presentation into an orientation program as a way to energize new employees on their first day of work.

Speaking of training, how can you make this process more engaging and interactive? Cultural change often requires employees to brush up on old skills and learn new ones, so think about how this experience could be improved from their perspective. Can they take an online course from home on their own time and be compensated upon completion? Is there a way to improve job-shadowing and hands-on training? Do a little research, but don't overthink it. At this stage, the goal is to foster an environment where information flows freely, and change is seen as a positive thing.

Observe

You can present the facts, give a great sales pitch and hope for the best, but at the end of the day, every employee will decide for themselves whether or not to buy into the new culture. Their opinions will be based on what they observe and believe to be real, regardless of what they are told.

Cultural change is like a mini revolution under your own roof, but you're the one in control. The secret to pulling this off is to build your army with trust instead of charisma or fear. You and your management team must be the first ones to embrace the change and present a united front, because after all, if the guys calling the shots don't care, why should anyone else?

Consistency is the name of the game because everybody is watching– always! Your employees are observing your every move, waiting and subconsciously hoping you slip up. It's not that they're bad people, but your failure will validate their resistance to change. To prevent this from happening, you'll need to drum up every ounce of self-discipline to stay on track until your own actions become habits. Doing so will add to your own credibility, and set the stage for a real movement to occur.

Like I said, every employee must cross this imaginary line for themselves, and their decision comes from a place of trust. If they believe the change is real, permanent and everybody is moving forward with it, they will have no choice but to adopt the new culture. However, any inconsistencies between what is said and done, or even inconsistencies between different authoritative figures, will lead to speculation and mistrust. And the last thing you want to do during this transition is give your employees ammunition against you and your cause.

Leading by example is the only sure way to change somebody's perspective, particularly when new employees are introduced into the organization. It's well known that peak engagement occurs within the first ninety days of employment, but bear in mind that their first impression will form in a matter of minutes. While a solid training program is an absolute must to communicate the correct attitude and behaviors, in reality, new employees will absorb and emulate whatever they observe first hand.

Do

After the new rules of the game are established, and the employee deems it necessary to change their own behavior, the real work comes with practice, practice, practice. Habitual change isn't pretty; it's a gritty process of wins, setbacks, highs, and lows. It can be a tedious, uphill battle for both the trainer and trainee, so keeping team morale high is a necessity.

Focusing on the right things starts with an appreciation that some of us adapt to change better than others. In fact, dealing with change (or even just thinking about it) can bring on intense anxiety for some people. It's not their fault, nor is it something that can be avoided– it's just how they're hardwired.

Anxiety can take on many forms, such as a loss of confidence, stress, panic or fear. It can affect performance and lead to otherwise avoidable mistakes, creating a self-perpetuating cycle of tension. It's highly unlikely your employees will come right out and say they're anxious about change, so like a shepherd, you'll have to vigilantly watch for anyone straying from the group and guide them back.

In these circumstances, your best option is to build their self-confidence with open communication and positive reinforcement, beginning with the acknowledgment of their own feelings. You may need to dangle a carrot if the employee is reluctant to open up, by either stating what you've observed or sharing a personal story that's relevant to the situation. If they can identify what's bothering them and talk it out with somebody they trust, the problem will become less scary. Be sure to keep the conversation going throughout the entire process, celebrating wins and cheering them on while they navigate through this difficult time.

Employees may also face physical barriers with respect to their own personality and skills. For example, if an introverted salesperson is now tasked with being more assertive and outgoing, this could present a serious challenge for them. They might understand and agree with the necessary changes, but still be uncomfortable with it nonetheless.

Empathy plays a pivotal role in these instances, where you intentionally take a step back and see things from their perspective. The typical *here's what needs to be done, so do it* approach doesn't work because the objective goes against who they are and their conventional way of doing things. Instead, they need concentrated, on-the-spot feedback to reinforce the right behavior every step along the way, accompanied with the same encouragement we just discussed.

Fear of the unknown is what keeps people clinging to the past, even as they're reaching out for what's in front of them. Resistance and regression come from a place of safety, not malice, and as the leader, it's your job to reassure everyone that you'll get through this together. Eventually, they'll come around, and their success will become your own.

A FEW TIPS TO GET YOU STARTED

Cultural change is anything but romantic, especially when you consider that total transformation could take up to two years to take root. But don't get discouraged, there are plenty of things you can do right out of the gate to improve your culture and get others on your side.

Tell Stories

Storytelling is the oldest and most effective form of communication. It can be entertaining, educational, comforting and for some, deeply personal. Storytelling also happens to be a strategic business tool to capture the attention of your audience and create emotional bonds. Likewise, when facts and figures are presented through this creative medium, the audience can visualize the information and store it for easy recollection.

This is my favorite way to onboard new employees, but there was a time when I dreaded this process.

The very first orientation program I put together was in retrospect, pretty awful. We used to hold our new employees hostage for several hours and force-feed them bullet points from a mundane PowerPoint presentation. It wouldn't take long for them to tune out, and when they did, it was glaringly obvious: doodling on the page, yawning, glassy eyes, the whole bit. Honestly, I couldn't even blame them because it was just as painful for me, and I was the presenter!

This charade continued for a year or two until I picked up on a strategy commonly used during Ted Talks and other high-profile keynotes. Regardless of their background, experience, and message, nearly every speaker had one thing in common: they were all master storytellers. They had an idea to share, but instead of ramming it down our throats they chose to lead us through an emotional journey. The concept was new to me, but with a little research, I discovered this was common knowledge among the experts. I was sold on the idea and excited to give it a try for myself.

Shortly after that, my new presentation was ready to go. Sixty slides were whittled down to just twelve with nothing more than a picture for each. I scrapped my theoretical situations for real-life examples of superior service and teamwork. I'll admit I was a little nervous about its reception, but when the big day came, I was blown away.

Not only did I hold their attention for the full hour, but they were actually engaged! There was smiling, laughter, questions and commentary. They hung onto my every word and silently acknowledged my points with head nodding. However, my excitement truly peaked a few months later when some of these stories made their rounds on their own accord. It was the validation I needed to prove the system worked and what I had to say was important.

So that's one of my success stories, what are yours?

Start with the Easiest Employees

When it comes to creating buy-in, seeing is believing. It only takes a handful of ambassadors to get the rest of the group on board, so it only makes sense to seek out the easiest people first. These are typically your newest employees, who are eager to please, as well as anyone within your inner circle and upper management.

As for the bottom 20% who are a pain in your butt, those who firmly believe you can't teach an old dog new tricks, don't waste your time on them. They'll either conform out of necessity because they value their job, or they'll show themselves the door if management doesn't beat them to the punch. Focus your time and energy on the employees who care and natural selection will take care of the rest.

Make it Fun

I can tell you first hand that plunking children down in front of their dinner and issuing an ultimatum doesn't work very well. And yet when I make it entertaining, and shift their focus away from their concerns, the meal is quickly gobbled up and the requests for seconds come pouring in. That's right, cultural change is just like getting your kids to eat their veggies.

Think of all the ways you can encourage the right behavior while making it fun. Measurable goals can be masked as friendly competitions, like who can answer the most phone calls or close the most deals each day. Contest prizes should be simple and fun – nothing too serious that will create hard feelings.

Peer Recognition

This is also a big part of the implementation process. It feels just as good to give praise as it does to receive it, and encouraging others to see the good in their colleagues will eventually wash away past grievances. Consider holding an event where staff fill out appreciation notes for one another, find reasons to have cake or throw a pizza party. It doesn't really matter what it is, so long as it feels like a celebration and brings the group closer together.

* * *

If this chapter was more theoretical than you bargained for, I can assure you this was done intentionally. Organizational culture is a crucial component to any business, and sadly a topic often oversimplified and misunderstood. The most important takeaway here is that the foundation of your business must be viewed through multiple lenses to ensure all your bases are covered. The chain always breaks at the weakest link, and in this case, it's wherever your expectations are not understood and met.

From this point on, everything we discuss will be a practical guide requiring actual work on your part. The fluffy talk is over, and it's about to get real. In the next chapter, we'll create your company's Vision and Mission Statements, so grab a pen and paper, and let's get started.

Chapter 11

VISION AND MISSION STATEMENTS

Vision and mission (VM) statements are powerful tools to communicate the organization's aspirations, values, and commitments. They can be used internally to onboard new recruits and pull the team together, or externally to publicly declare the company's intent and create brand awareness. I've found people are rarely indifferent to VM statements – they either love or hate them.

For those who see VM statements as a fad or pointless bureaucracy, I get it. Here's the problem: most people don't fully understand them, including a number of large corporations. They're confusing; thanks to the various experts who use the terms interchangeably. They're meaningless because companies intentionally make them sound fluffy. They're superficial because the same organizations say one thing and do another.

Or maybe you have your own reasons for not implementing them in your business. You're too busy, too small, too big, or whatever excuse is popular this week. You've survived this long without them, so *if it ain't broke, why fix it?*

That's one perspective, but here's another.

Movie producers use trailers to market their films. Authors include a synopsis on the back of their book and recording artists release singles ahead of their album. Even manufacturers like Apple or Tesla hold extravagant launch events well ahead of their product's release date. You could say all of this is a ploy to create buzz and capture sales, and while true, there's more to it than that.

Regardless of the industry or approach, the fundamental goal is the same: to get the product in the hands of the right people – their target audience. The truth is, you can't sell everything to everyone, and if you try, the majority of people will always be disappointed. Genres exist for this very reason – they lay out the expectations up front. Some people like action movies and heavy metal, while others prefer romantic comedies and country music. You can't please everyone – it's just not going to happen.

The beauty of marketing is that it takes the guesswork out of the equation. It only takes a three-minute clip to decide whether or not the movie is right for you. When you read the back of the book, you'll either open it up or place it back on the shelf. It all comes down to attracting the right customer and minimizing the odds they'll be left disappointed, because when they are it's a much tougher sell the next time around.

Obviously, there are no guarantees that a good preview equates to a good movie. I hate finding out the hard way that all the good parts were in the trailer, or that the single is the only good song on the entire album. It feels like I was duped out of twenty bucks and it leaves a bad taste in my mouth. So does this mean all previews are bad? Of course not, and the same holds true for VM statements.

People naturally gravitate toward organizations they trust and identify with. Some will answer the call and help bring the leader's vision to life, while others will simply adopt the brand as a consumer. Every leader is inherently responsible for the cohesion between themselves, their team, and the outside world, but this becomes increasingly difficult as the business grows beyond the leader's immediate sphere of influence.

There are many companies out there with fantastic VM statements, relentlessly marketing themselves to attract the right people to their business. When the puzzle pieces fit properly, everybody wins. In this chapter, we'll cover everything you need to know about vision and mission statements, including how to create them and put them to good use.

VISION STATEMENTS

A vision statement is a plan for the future, articulating whatever dreams and aspirations the leader conceives. It sets the tone for what the organization will ultimately become in terms of its values, obligations, and growth, firmly establishing a foundation with unlimited possibilities.

At the very heart of any vision statement is the answer to why: why the company exists and why anyone should care. When the organization's why is understood, it forms a shared sense of purpose within the group and inspires others to contribute to a greater good. An authentic vision statement builds trust, giving others something to believe in and get behind.

MISSION STATEMENTS

A mission statement is a call to action focused on the present, clarifying who the organization serves and what's required to fulfill the leader's vision. It also serves as the company's guiding light to ensure decisions are aligned with its goals and public image. An effective mission statement defines what success looks like and rallies the troops to present a united front.

THE GOOD, THE BAD AND THE UGLY

In a recent study[2] researchers analyzed VM statements of the leading U.S. companies listed in the Fortune 500, ranking their effectiveness based on the content and clarity of their message. It revealed that only 154 of the 500 firms provided clearly-defined vision statements, and of these, only 37% contained quality content from a visionary perspective. Even more troubling, nearly half of the listed companies didn't provide any form of statement describing their vision, mission, and purpose, confirming the lack of consistency between use, content and delivery among the corporate elite.

So what does this say about VM statements? At a glance, they appear to be irrelevant to the success of the company since they are, after all, listed on the

---

[2] Kasowski, Bart and Louise Jacques Filion. "A Study of the 2005 Fortune 500 Vision Statements." (HEC Montréal, 2010).

Fortune 500. But then again, I suppose this depends on how you define success. If success is merely profits and sustainability, then there's validity to the previous claim. But if you also consider other factors such as brand awareness and consumer loyalty, I would argue that VM statements play a significant role.

Choose your preference: Pepsi or Coca-Cola, Ford or Chevrolet, Nike or Adidas, Apple or Microsoft. One thing we can agree on is that all of these wonderful brands have developed a cult-like following and lead the pack in their respective industries. Each has a passionate following who will argue to the death over who has the better beverage or coolest gadget.

I'm not suggesting these companies dominate their markets because of their VM statements, but it's also no coincidence that all of them know exactly who they are and communicate what they believe.

So do you need a vision and mission statement to be profitable? Absolutely not, but if you want to be memorable, unique, and have a loyal following, then you may want to reconsider. Before we dive into creating our own VM statements, let's take a look at a few of the best and worst statements out there.

The Good: Vision Statements

Amazon

"Our vision is to be the earth's most customer centric company; to build a place where people can come to find and discover anything they might want to buy online."

Kiva

"We envision a world where all people – even in the most remote areas of the globe – hold the power to create opportunity for themselves and others."

Nike

"To bring inspiration and innovation to every athlete* in the the world. * If you have a body, you're an athlete."

Toys "R" Us

"Our vision is to put joy in kids' hearts and a smile on parents' faces."

First impression, love them! You get a true sense of their calling and why these companies exist. Their messages are elegantly simplistic and resonate on a personal level; we feel compelled to give back to the less-fortunate, inspired to improve our health, and have nostalgic flashbacks to our childhood. These vision statements do exactly what they are intended to do: communicate what the future looks like and move us toward action.

The Good: Mission Statements

Google

"To provide access to the world's information in one click."

Ben & Jerry's

"Making the best possible ice cream, in the nicest possible way."

Southwest Airlines

"The mission of Southwest Airlines is dedication to the highest quality of Customer Service delivered with a sense of warmth, friendliness, individual pride and Company Spirit."

Disney

"We create happiness by providing the finest entertainment for people of all ages, everywhere."

Again, these messages hit their mark by articulating what the organizations do, how they do it, and to whom do they do it for. They also define how employees are expected to act and make decisions, including the type of experience customers can expect in return.

These mission statements are particularly effective because they embody the values of the organization, not so much in what is said but how it feels. Southwest implies a family-friendly company without outright saying it, and we assume they treat their employees in the same manner as they treat their customers. This is a perfect example of how mission statements can be creatively worded so people can read between the lines and get a genuine feeling what the organization is all about.

The Bad and the Ugly

We won't spend too much time on these, but it's worth looking at a few poorly constructed statements to illustrate the do's and don'ts of content creation and delivery:

Albertson's

"Guided by relentless focus on our five imperatives, we will constantly strive to implement the critical initiatives required to achieve our vision. In doing this, we will deliver operational excellence in every corner of the Company and meet or exceed our commitments to the many constituencies we serve. All of our long-term strategies and short-term actions will be moulded by a set of core values that are shared by each and every associate."

Um, what? There's a long-winded description of imperatives, initiatives, vision, commitments, constituencies, strategies and actions, but nothing tangible about their organization. After a little investigative work, you'd discover they're a grocery chain, but judging by their mission statement, they could have been a mining company, a bank or just about anything else. In terms of employee direction, it's confusing, it's fluffy, and there's absolutely nothing of value here.

Caterpillar

"Be the global leader in customer value"

What is customer value anyway? I'm sure they'd be hard-pressed to come up with an answer because value is subjective. Some place value on price, others on service, or something else entirely. You can't tell an employee to get out there and give value, they need specific direction. I'll give Caterpillar credit for trying to keep it simple, but sadly this statement falls short of explaining anything useful about the company.

Over One Hundred Fortune 500 Companies

No official statement.

You may have the right to remain silent, but it's not necessarily the best way to do business. Yes, these companies are financially successful, well-established and don't need a formal statement to be profitable, but what about everyone on the inside? How do these organizations engage their employees, get everyone pointed in the right direction and inspire them to do great things?

Sadly, in most cases, they don't, and it shows on their employees' faces. I'm sure these companies will remain profit machines for years to come, but that doesn't translate to a pleasant customer experience and a healthy organizational culture.

THE VERDICT

Most companies struggle to communicate who they are and why they exist, creating a three-way void between themselves, their employees, and their customers. The takeaway here is that:

A Good Statement...	A Bad Statement...
✓ Is specific and clear	X Is vague and confusing
✓ Uses everyday language	X Uses jargon
✓ Is inspiring and actionable	X Is dry and meaningless
✓ Conveys emotion	X Is cold and factual
✓ Is unique and memorable	X Is generic and forgettable

So, what's it going to be? Share your vision, outline your expectations, and build a loyal following, or cross your fingers and hope everyone figures it out for themselves? Effective leaders know clarity wins hearts and minds, ambiguity does not.

CREATING YOUR OWN

Alright, you're finally ready to push off the dock and set sail. You'll need a pen, paper, and a clear head to get those creative juices flowing. Even if your business already has a vision and mission statement, purge everything from your mind and start with a blank canvas. As a fun little experiment, use the steps below to create something fresh and see how they compare to the original. You can always keep whatever feels right, or throw everything back into the melting pot and give it another stir.

YOUR VISION STATEMENT

Step 1: Discover Your Why

It's assumed that every organization wants to be successful, but they shouldn't be in business just to make a buck. Your why defines who you are and why your company actually exists. What are you passionate about, what interests you? Are you driven to help people? Do you enjoy being innovative and solving problems? What is it that you love to do, and which changes would you like to see? This is your why.

Write down a few versions and then revise them into a single sentence. Don't worry about perfecting your message, as it will get reworked into your vision statement shortly. What's most important is that your answer is authentically you.

As for me, my why is **to help entrepreneurs break down barriers and execute their vision.**

Step 2: Dream Big

Now's the time to make that crazy, ambitious list of all the things you'd like to be and accomplish. Where do you see yourself in the next ten years and which opportunities are out there for future growth? Who are your customers, and what additional products and services will you offer them? This is a brainstorming session, so have fun with it and don't be afraid to dream big.

I envisioned an online community to complement this program; a place where entrepreneurs could find additional resources and support throughout their journey. Everybody's situation is different, and the most important thing for me was that everyone crossed the finish line.

It goes without saying, but don't include being rich and famous; this is merely a byproduct of your hard work. Instead, frame your dreams around specific things you can do to be successful.

If you're stumped or looking for more inspiration, tap into the ideas of a few trusted members of your inner circle to gain additional perspectives. It's also a good idea to look at what other industry leaders are doing, do a little reverse engineering and add your own twist. In particular, pay close attention to how they engage both their customers and employees.

Step 3: Boil It Down

Ok, this is actually a two-step process to distill your ideas into the essence of your vision. First, you'll need to run your list through a series of filters to separate the good stuff from the junk:

Scrap everything unrelated to the business. Recreational activities, personal goals and interests have nothing to do with vision statements.

Personal, work-related goals can also get tossed if they don't influence the behavior of your customers and employees. For example, dedicating an hour each day to get caught up on emails and paperwork should be removed from your list, but committing the same time to engage your team and talk to customers is ok.

Vision statements are timeless, and the work is never done, so eliminate tasks that won't impact the longevity of the business (excluding charitable work). This includes to-do lists, company projects and mandates with a finite end date.

Good job, but you're not done yet. Based on everything that's left over, how would you summarize your vision for the future? Write one sentence as if you were describing it to your employees, and another as if you were presenting it to your customers. When you're happy with both, merge them into a single sentence and clean it up.

After boiling down my own dream, I ended up with **to help entrepreneurs become a success story.**

Step 4: Apply the Why

Remember, effective vision statements are a call to action and trigger an emotional response. To invoke this type of reaction, your message must be infused with passion and purpose so it speaks to the heart. Here's how you do it.

Transfer your vision statement to the top of a fresh piece of paper, and below it, your *why*. Read both statements a few times out loud, then take a moment to reflect on what you're actually saying. The plan is to combine your philosophies and rewrite your vision statement once more, but this time in a way so others understand your true purpose.

The golden rule is to keep it simple, inspiring, and memorable so others will cling to it. Playful wording is a great way to achieve this, so long as the actual content of your message doesn't get lost in translation. Come up with a few versions, narrow it down and finalize your initial draft.

My Vision: To help entrepreneurs become a success story.

My Why: To help entrepreneurs break down barriers and execute their vision.

I thought more about the idea of a story arc, and how every hero encounters conflict throughout their journey. There are ups and downs along the way, but eventually the hero levels up and wins the day. In my case, I had the opportunity to help others write the outcome to their own story.

Therefore, my final vision statement became ***to help entrepreneurs build a business and a life they love.***

Step 5: Speak and Polish

The final step is to iron out the wrinkles and ensure your message is crystal clear. Read your vision statement out loud with the same projection and confidence as if you were speaking to a crowd. Repeat this a few times until your delivery is fluid, then consider how the audience would interpret your message:

- o Does it paint a picture of the future that's intriguing and raise additional questions?

- o Does it sound natural or is it overly wordy and complex?

- o Is it engaging and memorable, or flat and forgettable?

- o Is it easily understood why your company exists?

LESS IS MORE!

Focus your vision around a single idea and keep it as simple as possible. Avoid generalizations, clichés, technical jargon, and corporate-speak.

Experiment with different wording and continue to polish your statement until it can be said with ease. As a final test, practice your vision statement on friends and family and have them describe back to you what your company is all about.

YOUR MISSION STATEMENT

Step 1: Define the How

Begin by writing down what behaviors are necessary to fulfill your vision. If you're in the service industry, you'll probably need to be friendly and level-headed. If you're in a professional industry such as medicine or law, trustworthiness and confidence are an absolute must. Write down six adjectives which best describe your ideal employee.

Now visualize what the perfect customer experience looks like from an outside perspective. What are their expectations and how can you exceed them? What draws them to your business, and describe their first impression when they walk through the doors? How does the quality of service compare over the phone or online? Compile your list of ideas and include any additional behaviors necessary to get the job done.

Your *how* is also the secret sauce of your business – the bells and whistles which make you the favorable choice over the competition. Say you want pizza delivered to your home, where do you order from? If you have rowdy kids and need it fast, you'll probably go with the *thirty minutes or it's free* guys because that's where you place your value. If you're a pizza connoisseur in search of the highest quality, you'll be swayed by anyone using fresh ingredients and a wood-burning stove. Pizza venues offering a *two for one* price strategy position themselves as the economical choice. Consider your own *how* and what special things your company does to make itself stand out and to be the obvious front-runner.

Similar to your vision statement, it's time to pull everything together and summarize your *how*. This is only the first step, so it doesn't have to be perfect, just keep in mind the emphasis isn't on what you do, but how you do it.

Remember, my vision is **to help entrepreneurs build a business and a life they love.** How am I going to do this? By teaching entrepreneurs how to build their dream team.

Step 2: Define the What

Zig Ziglar famously remarked, "People don't buy drills, they buy holes." I've always loved this idea and use a similar example in one of my training seminars, where a customer is in need of a toilet. In this case, the solution involves multiple products, including a wax seal, bolts, caulking, a wrench, and typically a new seat.

This doesn't even take into account the type of toilet they need, their budget, and the expertise to either install it or guide them through the process. In other words, we don't sell products and services, we sell solutions and experiences– the total package. This is your *what*.

When it comes to communicating your *what,* it's important to be specific enough, so the outside world understands what it is you do, without creating boundaries and inhibiting future growth. In the previous example, Caterpillar's quest to be the "global leader in customer value" is too vague and generic – we don't know what it is they do or provide, so we lose interest.

Disney on the other hand "creates happiness," which perfectly describes everything they do without restricting future expansion. They produce theatrical, television and music entertainment, operate the world's most successful theme parks and resorts and are the masters of merchandise and distribution. However, they've chosen to sell *happiness* to their customers, which will continue to describe the future endeavors of Disney.

Start your sentence with "We create" or "We provide" and get creative with it, but above all else, be sure your *what* is aligned with the company's vision and values to avoid confusion.

At All-Star Academy, **we provide a step-by-step guide how to clone yourself and automate your business.**

Step 3: Define the Who

Easy but often overlooked, your mission statement should specify who the organization ultimately serves. The *who* further clarifies the purpose of the company, keeps your message customer-focused, and verifies their needs have actually been met.

Again, for me, I'm focused on anyone who's struggling to grow their business and live the life they've envisioned.

Additional points to consider are the responsibilities the organization has to its employees, community, and environment. For example, if you're committed to minimizing your carbon footprint, you may wish to include this in your mission statement, providing, of course, this is actually happening. If family values are important, you could add something that humanizes your company and promotes a nurturing, supportive environment. While this is certainly not required, it does add a level of authenticity to the company and is an effective way to attract other people who share the same beliefs as you.

Step 4: Write, Speak, and Polish

Once again, pull everything together and this time clearly state how the vision will be accomplished, what will be done and for whom. Just like the vision statement, keep it clean and interesting. Write, speak, polish and repeat until you have it down to a single sentence.

My How: To teach entrepreneurs how to build their team

My What: We provide a step-by-step guide to clone yourself and automate your business.

My Who: Anyone struggling to grow their business

My final mission statement eventually became *to teach entrepreneurs how to build their dream team and automate their business.*

Quick Tips:

- o Make it unique and memorable

- o Avoid anything to do with profitability, efficiency, and rewards

- o Ensure it's measurable, scalable, and realistic

- o Make it global, something everyone can get behind regardless of their role

NEXT STEPS

VM statements aren't very useful on their own, and like any other tool, they must be properly used to get the most out of them. Below are some recommendations on how you can best utilize your newly created statements:

- o Display in high-traffic areas where customers and staff will most likely read them

- o Display on your website

- o Add to your email signature, business cards and company letterhead

- o Incorporate into your training programs and resources

- o Recite at the beginning or end of regularly scheduled staff meetings

- o Reward employees who can recite them when randomly asked

- o Most importantly, live them daily and lead by example

I can say with confidence that VM statements helped our family business level up. At one time, our company felt like the Wild West, where it was every man and woman for themselves. Our employees all had different reasons for being there, different ambitions and varying work ethics.

But after we formalized our VM statements and shared them with our staff, everything fell into place. Suddenly, there was a collective sense of purpose, transforming our employees into an actual team. Those who were on board adopted the universal responsibility to help one another succeed, while the non-team players were quick to show themselves the door.

Everything got better after everyone understood that we were all on the same side and working toward a common goal. Office politics became virtually nonexistent, our productivity and profitability went up, not to mention my own proficiencies as a leader. With a clear picture of the future, it became significantly easier to train my team and measure results.

Nothing compares to the feeling of having people come together to adopt your vision and mission as their own. It's pretty incredible when you think about it.

Chapter 12

CORE VALUES

Our core values are the foundation of our belief system and the guiding principles we instinctively adhere to. In fact, these values are so deeply ingrained in our being they can manifest into physical form. That undeniable gut feeling we've all experienced is our core values hard at work, acting as our moral compass to distinguish right from wrong and help filter our decisions.

History is filled with ordinary people who became exceptional leaders simply because they communicated what they believed. They captivated audiences with not only the magnitude of their words but also how they lived their lives according to their values. People were willing to trust these figures because they saw something in them that they recognized in themselves, and were inspired to follow in the footsteps of their new, silently-appointed leader.

Even right now, within your own organization, exists the same laws of nature. Broadcasting your vision and values will attract the right people into your circle of influence – those who will bring the company's mission to life and stick around for the long haul. But communicating your values plays another crucial role, one that affects virtually every aspect of your business.

The truth is that even with a healthy culture, robust training program and the best team at your disposal, there's still a chance you'll fall short of your goals and have underperforming employees. And believe me, I can tell you firsthand how frustrating it feels to be doing everything by the book and still not get the results you'd hoped for. So what's the deal?

Intentional or not, most companies rely on rules and fear tactics to influence behavior. Throwing a policy manual at your employees is basically saying, "Don't screw up or we'll catch you," which isn't a great way to empower them and build their confidence. But as we all know, most policies aren't black and white, and so whenever an employee encounters an unfamiliar situation, they're just rolling the dice to see if they've solved the problem or accentuated it.

When company values are introduced and communicated in the right way, **you're training your employees how to think, instead of how to act.** When their personal values are aligned with those of the company, decisions become easy regardless of experience and training. Similarly, when the organization's focus shifts from governing laws to guiding decisions, employees feel safe to make bold decisions and take calculated risks in the same manner as you would.

There are core values you live by, even if they don't easily come to mind. So, before you can apply them to your business, they must be formalized in writing and in a manner which speaks to the heart.

THE PROCESS

Establishing a core set of values is instrumental in shaping the right organizational culture, but this must come directly from you, the leader. This isn't something that can be delegated off to your human resources department or developed with a company-wide poll. The objective isn't to build a consensus among the group, but instead, pass along the fundamental values to your team who will carry out your vision.

This is a process of personal reflection and discovery, and while it's tempting to arbitrarily choose fancy words from a thesaurus, remember that your ability to inspire and build trust relies on a message just as unique as you.

Before we get started, let's take a moment to appreciate what an effective set of company values looks like. Southwest Airlines, an American airline and the world's largest low-cost carrier[3], is considered by many experts to be a leading authority in the development of organizational culture.

---

[3] "Southwest Airlines," Wikipedia. https://en.wikipedia.org/wiki/Southwest_Airlines.

Principles of Living the Southwest Way[4]

Warrior Spirit

- Work Hard
- Display a sense of urgency
- Desire to be the best

- Persevere
- Be courageous
- Innovate

A Servant's Heart

- Follow the Golden Rule
- Demonstrate proactive customer service

- Treat others with respect
- Put others first
- Embrace the Southwest Family

Fun-LUVing Attitude

- Have FUN
- Be a passionate team player
- Don't take yourself too seriously

- Celebrate successes
- Maintain perspective
- Enjoy your work

Southwest Airlines does an excellent job of balancing empowerment with accountability. They encourage employees to pursue excellence and personal growth, while at the same time, specifying how their performance is measured. It doesn't matter if you're an employee or customer, Southwest Airlines spells out the experience you can expect.

These are their values, and you have yours, so let's dive into the creative process.

---

[4] "Principles of Living the Southwest Way," 2011 Southwest Airlines One Report. http://www.southwestonereport.com/2011/#!/people/employees/one-luv.

Step 1: Start with a Clean Slate

There's no sense holding on to the past, so throw out all of your preconceived notions about yourself, your customers, your business, everything! The focus is on what you actually believe, not what you *think* you believe. Take a deep breath, stretch out your legs and clear your mind. Remember this is a process of discovery, so don't force anything that isn't 100% you.

Step 2: Mind Map

Consider the following questions about your business:

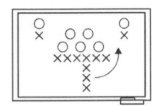

- o How do we treat our customers?
- o How do we treat each other?
- o How will we grow and prosper?
- o How do we wish to be perceived?

For each question, start writing down whatever comes to mind. It can be a single word, a sentence, a personal experience or an emotion, just get it all out and write, write, write! It doesn't have to sound pretty, or even be coherent for that matter, at this point, it's all about creating content. Think about your favorite places to shop, eat or be entertained, and the details that go into making that experience feel special. What can you do to emulate those feelings within your business?

Step 3: Divide and Conquer

Group your ideas into common themes such as customer service, teamwork, and personal development, then determine the best word or phrase for each. There's no magic number you're shooting for, other than having at least three or four to work with that do not overlap one another.

Step 4: Write, Speak & Polish

The key to crafting a solid set of values is to make them unique, specific and actionable. If you only have a few, phrase them in a playful, memorable way. If you're like Southwest Airlines and have quite a few, then follow their lead by dividing them into common threads with a catchy title.

Either way, keep them in the present tense and avoid using conditional phrases such as *We Strive To* or *We Try To*. Either do or don't, there's no room for trying when it comes to your values. Likewise, nothing kills your authenticity like an eye-rolling cliché, so avoid these at all costs.

Just as before with your VM statements, read them out loud and polish them to perfection.

Here's a list of our Core Values at All-Star Academy:

1. Lead with passion, integrity, and gratitude.

2. Treat everyone like family.

3. Help others reach their full potential.

4. Welcome and inspire change.

5. Make valuable mistakes.

6. Learn, share, and grow everyday.

Step 5: Put them to the Test

The final step is to test their integrity- and yours! Once again, consider the following questions, this time looking for anything vague, wordy, confusing or contradictory to what you actually believe and do:

o   Do they firmly represent what I believe, regardless of my industry?

o   Do they clearly articulate the expected behaviors and mindset?

o   Do they empower others to grow and excel? Are they engaging?

o   Are they consistent with organization's vision and mission statements?

When every value has made the cut, give yourself a high-five and take a moment to reflect on what you've accomplished. You've officially established your company's core ideologies and tied them into your vision and mission, enabling everyone on your team to make better decisions and be more consistent with their behavior. Up next, we'll weave everything together into an easy-to-remember mantra.

Chapter 13

WHY A MANTRA MATTERS

It's your first day on the job, working for an organization you know little about. You partake in the orientation program and are given a thorough explanation of the company's culture: VM statements, core values, stories and examples, the whole kit and caboodle. The presentation ends on a high note, and while you're feeling inspired to jump right in, there's a problem – you're in complete information overload.

Even with an orientation program worthy of a standing ovation, most employees are going to walk away feeling a little foggy and unable to recall at least half of what was discussed. And fair enough, it's a lot of information to take in for anyone, let alone somebody who's new and is already anxious about starting a new job.

Company mantras are one of the most underrated tools at your disposal, and when used correctly, can bridge the gap between communication and comprehension. It's a unique phrase that embodies the organization's philosophies, so they can be easily understood and recalled at a moment's notice.

The applications for a mantra go far beyond the onboarding process, and truthfully, are most effective as part of the organization's regular operations. They advise employees to prioritize tasks, think for themselves and trust their own judgment. I often refer to our mantra during spontaneous coaching sessions and team meetings to maintain top-of-mind awareness. Additionally, I use it for myself to keep my own actions in check to ensure I practice what I preach.

Google once embraced the clever mantra *Don't Be Evil* to summarize everything they believed[5]. They still had a vision and mission statement, including a variety of values and leadership principles, but *Don't Be Evil* is what they wanted you to remember. After Google's transition to Alphabet, the slogan was replaced with, *Do the Right Thing*, which was equally effective at communicating what they believed.

CREATING YOUR OWN

Your mantra doesn't have to be witty or sophisticated, even something as simple as, *Make People Happy* or *Safety, Quality, Professionalism* are acceptable. Review your vision, mission, and values, then write down the top 4 or 5 words that best describe your organization.

At All-Star Academy, our mantra is **Let it Go to Let it Grow**, which embodies everything we believe and do. Obviously, the practices we teach to automate your business involve letting go of failures, fear, and responsibility as part of the cloning process, but the mantra works internally as well. It's a way to keep all of us in check and ensure personal interests do not inhibit the success of our company and clients.

Keep the following in mind as you create your own mantra:

o   Keep it short and sweet

o   Choose actionable words

o   Be sure it reflects a specific mindset and relatable behaviors

o   Make it memorable

With a defined Vision, Mission, Values and Mantra, we can now turn our attention to the company's local culture beginning with Performance Standards.

---

[5] Wall Street Journal Blog, The. "Google's 'Don't' Be Evil' Becomes Alphabet's 'Do the Right Thing'. https://blogs.wsj.com/digits/2015/10/02/as-google-becomes-alphabet-dont-be-evil-vanishes/.

Chapter 14

PERFORMANCE STANDARDS

You and I are best friends, we love pizza, and every Friday is pizza day. We walk into a new restaurant not knowing what to expect, and behold, we have the best experience of our life! Delicious food, impeccable service, a fun and relaxing atmosphere – everything is perfect. So next Friday when we go out for pizza, where do you think we are going? We're heading back of course, why wouldn't we?

The following week we return to the same restaurant but leave utterly disappointed. They messed up our order twice, the waitress was a little snobby, and the tables were disgusting. It's fair to assume the next time we're in the mood for pizza, we're taking our business elsewhere.

Ok, so let's say that didn't happen and in fact, our second, third, fourth and fifth visits were just as amazing. We love this place, but unfortunately, on the sixth visit, we really do have a subpar experience. Maybe it wasn't as dramatic as the example before, but the service was bad. Now think about this long and hard for a moment, where are you *actually* going to go the next time you want pizza?

Unless you're an impossible person to please, I'd bet you're probably going to go back and give it another shot. Why? Because consistency is like building a little slush fund, and the more positive experiences your customers have, the more they are willing to forgive the occasional slip up.

So let's assume we return for pizza every Friday for the next six months, and then out of the blue, a new pizza restaurant opens up across the street. Where we will go this time?

Again, if we're being completely honest, there's a high probability we'll check it out because we can't help ourselves. Even though we have everything we want, we create a false sense of missing out in our mind. And so, we temporarily set aside our loyalty and check out the new place.

Now, this is where the true power of consistency can either make or break your business. The competition is undoubtedly positioned as the new and exciting alternative choice but also faces the disadvantage of having to meet, let alone exceed, the expectations of the preferred venue. The quality of the food, service, and atmosphere must be at the very least on par because that's what we've come to expect; and if they fail to deliver, we're heading right back. Sure, they might be cheaper or have some novelty which permanently steals a small percentage of customers, but you and I, along with many others, will eventually return to our favorite place.

So the lesson here is that consistency:

✓ Ensures the first impression is the right one

✓ Secures repeat business for the future

✓ Creates a slush fund for trust and forgiveness

✓ Raises the bar for the competition

Consistency is the X-factor which differentiates industry leaders from everybody else. It's the goal of every business, but achieving and maintaining consistency is one of the greatest challenges faced by any leader. To accomplish this, you'll need to implement certain measures to protect the company from damaging behavior, and work diligently to deliver the top-notch service that keeps your customers coming back for more.

PERFORMANCE STANDARDS

Standards are the non-negotiable expectations of the leader – the line drawn in the sand, so to speak. They are specific, measurable objectives and policies demanding 100% compliance by everyone, at all times.

Using another pizza analogy, the *Delivery Within Thirty Minutes Or It's Free* gimmick is a standard. The policy is black and white: the customer gets everything they ordered in thirty minutes, period. Thirty minutes is the standard and the bare minimum level of performance. Getting it there in twenty-three minutes is great, but thirty-one is unacceptable.

Implementing performance standards was a game-changer for me. I had previously spent so much time regurgitating the same direction to my employees that I actually began to resent them. They did as they pleased with little concern for consequence, and in retrospect, it was my fault for not holding them accountable in the first place.

Enough was enough, and at some point, we decided to implement our first performance standard: show up to your workstation on time, in a clean uniform, with a smile on your face; common sense, right? Failure to meet this standard in any way would result in mandatory disciplinary action.

At first, our staff didn't take these new rules seriously, but that soon changed after we started issuing verbal warnings and suspensions. The list of standards grew to two, then five and ten, and before I knew it, our business was hopping, and I no longer had to repeat myself. The bar was set, and it was everybody's job to meet or exceed our expectations moving forward.

When it comes to performance standards, look no further than Disney. They're arguably the world's most successful company in terms of brand consistency, due to their impeccably high standards and rigorous training program. If you've been lucky enough to visit Disneyland, you'll know exactly what I'm talking about.

For a theme park averaging close to fifty thousand guests per day[6], you'll be hard-pressed to find garbage on the ground or a washroom in need of service. Their food is always fresh, merchandise stocked and well-displayed, and flowers individually cared for. It doesn't matter who's Cinderella or Mickey Mouse,

---

[6] "17 Mind-Boggling Statistics About the Disneyland Resort," Theme Park Tourist. http://www.themeparktourist.com/features/20140227/16405/17-mind-boggling-statistics-about-disneyland-resort.

everyone plays their part to a tee. Disney is associated with quality and people are willing to pay a premium for their products and services, which again is a testament to their standards and overall success.

TYPES OF PERFORMANCE STANDARDS

Performance standards are divided into two categories. First, we have **Universal Standards**, which are the company-wide expectations everyone must follow. These are things like arriving to work on time and following health and safety protocols. Universal standards typically receive the formal treatment, being documented in an employee handbook and communicated during orientation.

Next, we have **Regional Standards** which are exclusive to a particular department or position. These tend to focus more on the quality and efficiency of the employee's work, as well as other mandates such as dress codes or certification prerequisites. Regional standards are occasionally documented in supplementary training material, but more often are verbally communicated and reinforced on the spot by management.

THE PROCESS

Depending on the health, size, and stability of your business, you may want to include your team as you come up with a list of performance standards. The benefit of inclusion is that the consensus will come from *their ideas*, meaning your employees will be more inclined to take ownership of them.

Secondly, when creating regional standards, they may have more expertise than yourself in certain areas and can contribute to finding the best solution. But if your team is struggling, it's probably best to work independently and bring them into the loop later.

To complete this process in its entirety, the following procedure would be conducted once for the company's universal standards and again for every region. Since your clone's primary focus is on the bigger picture, universal standards is where we'll begin. Don't worry about regional standards for the time being, they can be addressed later on after the cloning process is behind you.

Step 1: Identify Critical Functions

Critical functions are the most important things you do to make your customers happy. What do your customers expect from you and where do they place the most value? What makes you unique and stand out from the competition? Consider the various points of customer contact, and for each, write down the critical functions that influence their experience.

If you were operating a hotel, for example, there would certainly be expectations surrounding privacy, safety, comfort, and hospitality. As for the critical functions, check-in, housekeeping, room service, dining, parking, and concierge would be logical places to start.

Step 2: Determine the Success Criteria

Next, attach the measurable components to each critical function by clarifying the minimum expectation for compliance. There are six variables which can be used in any combination to define a performance standard:

Quality	The accuracy of the work and degree of excellence.
Quantity	The amount of work produced.
Timeliness	Deadlines for when the work must be complete.
Cost-Effectiveness	The minimal resources needed to produce the work.
Safety	Measures to minimize the risk of danger.
Conduct	Employee behavior aligned with the core values.

Once again, using the hotel as our example, we could list our standards for housekeeping:

Quality	Fully cleaned, restocked, and repaired
Quantity	75% of all rooms
Timeliness	3:00 pm

Step 3: Write, Speak, & Polish

This process should feel pretty familiar by now. Craft your statements, speak them out loud and revise until you're satisfied.

Therefore, our final revision could read: *75% of the rooms must be ready for check-in by 3:00 pm.*

Experiment with different wording, so your performance standards are clear and concise but still general enough to minimize potential loopholes. *Ready for check-in* defines the end result and encompasses obvious duties such as cleaning and restocking, as well as any unforeseen tasks like maintenance.

Step 4: Organize and Prioritize

Thus far, we've approached performance standards from the company's perspective, but now we need to repackage them for the benefit of your employees. Compliance requires understanding, and in particular, how to make the right decision when things aren't black and white.

Having at least a dozen performance standards is by no means unreasonable, but nevertheless, could be somewhat overwhelming for your team when presented as a laundry list. A policy handbook is a great referral tool for both training and enforcing standards, but it's still no guarantee employees will make the right decision.

Alternatively, you can remove the ambiguity by categorizing and prioritizing your standards ahead of time, so there's no question what must be done. This may change depending on your business, but here's a suggested format to follow, prioritized from top to bottom:

Safety Standards: Regulations and best practices.

Team Standards: Codes of Conduct.

Service Standards: Deadlines for when the work must be complete.

Efficiency Standards: Policies and procedures to maximize profit.

Health and Safety Standards are always the top priority and can't be compromised for any reason. Next come **Team Standards** which promote a healthy organizational culture, followed by **Service Standards** which revolve around the customer experience. Finally, we have **Efficiency Standards** intended to maximize profitability. I'm a firm believer that people come before profits, and when you look after them, they'll look after your bottom line for you.

So let's back things up for a second because you're probably wondering why Team Standards are above Service Standards. Well to be blunt, **the needs of your team come before the needs of your customers.**

There I said it, now allow me to explain.

Obviously, taking care of your customers is one of the most important things you do, but exactly how do you plan on doing this if the organization's culture is toxic? When companies place customers ahead of their own employees, the message reads loud and clear: anyone is replaceable if they don't pull their weight. It's the classic *boss* mentality which employs fear tactics to get results at the expense of team morale.

But when employees come first, everything falls into place as it should. Employees who feel valued are more productive, efficient and happy. They lend a helping hand and go the extra mile because they care. They put the needs of the group ahead of their own self-interests because they believe it's the right thing to do. In a roundabout way, taking care of your team ensures they produce their best work to fulfill the leader's vision, at which point superior customer service becomes effortless.

ONE MORE THING

If the concept of performance standards is completely foreign to your team, the last thing you want to do is overwhelm them with a list of criteria and start demanding results. Every business is different, but remember, there's always going to be an adjustment period during cultural implementation where employees must understand, then observe, and eventually do. This means setting appropriate timelines for compliance and developing an action plan to get there.

You don't boil a frog by dropping it into a pot of boiling water because the frog will instinctively jump out. But if you place the frog in tepid water and slowly bring it to a boil, the gradual change in temperature will, for the most part, go unnoticed. The same philosophy should be applied to performance standards, especially in situations where an about-face is in order.

It's tempting to roll out the list, have the tough talk and start holding people accountable, but rarely do these situations play out the same way we had envisioned. In reality, some people will get on board right away but most won't, or not for the long haul anyway. With different personalities, abilities, motives, and levels of commitment, there's already a lot of variables to contend with; and for every standard introduced in parallel, the degree of difficulty increases by the same factor.

If the real goal is to achieve consistency, then everyone must move forward at the same pace and help one another along the way. Start with one or two standards, set a deadline and begin the training process. As your team gains traction, introduce another standard, and then another until you reach your final destination. Before you know it, they'll have adopted the new way of doing things without even knowing you've turned up the heat.

BONUS TIP!

Start with your management team a few weeks prior to the company-wide roll out. Modelling the correct behavior in advance will add to the credibility of your mandate and expedite employee buy-in.

As always, it's imperative to tie your vision, mission and values into the training process to communicate the *why* behind the transition. Compliance is important, but consistency is the long-game and to achieve this requires a change in both their behavior patterns and belief system.

Alright, we're down to the final segment of the Cultural Framework, so let's move on to Service Guidelines and finish strong!

Chapter 15

SERVICE GUIDELINES

If performance standards are yin, then service guidelines would be yang, coming together to form the total customer experience. Both promote consistency and echo the company's vision, mission and values, and yet on their own seem to contradict one another's purpose and approach.

Performance standards address the customer's needs by controlling measurable results. There's only one right way of doing things, so being a part of the team means playing by the rules. Service guidelines, on the other hand, are a set of **best practices focused on giving the customer what they really want– impeccable service!** They describe how to make everyone feel like a VIP and provide a launchpad for personalized service. In other words, performance standards lay out the minimum expectations, while service guidelines suggest how to exceed them.

The truth is your customers don't need you, or anyone else for that matter. Nowadays, their needs can be satisfied virtually anywhere, by anyone and anytime, and your ability to fulfill them doesn't make you special, it just makes you an option. Your customers want to feel understood, valued, and respected, so much so, that they're even willing to pay a premium for it. We're all in the business of pleasing people, but unfortunately, many companies lose sight of this.

Every employee is an ambassador for the organization, particularly those who interact with customers on the front lines. If you consider the endless combination of employee skills, knowledge, and personality types, the customer's experience could play out a number of ways based on how the dice are rolled. So unless you're prepared to leave everything to chance, you'll need to equip your team with the fundamentals of outstanding customers service and empower them to exercise good judgment.

THE KISS OF DEATH

Encouraging employees to go the extra mile is pointless without first establishing the right environment for them to thrive. We have a vision but often set unrealistic expectations around it. We try to control every situation with a policy or procedure. Where there's a loop hole, we introduce another regulation. Where there's a gray area, we establish a flow. Eventually, there's so much red tape that it's impossible for them to move, and then we can't figure out why they won't take the initiative.

Suppressing individualism is the kiss of death for creativity and dashes any hopes of personalized service. If your team is to succeed on their own terms, they must be given the opportunity to explore their interests, innovate and overcome obstacles without intervention.

Service guidelines are a way of illustrating what superior customer service looks like while granting employees certain liberties to personalize the experience. Outgoing individuals may be charismatic and use humor to build rapport, while introverts could be sought after for their expertise and attention to detail.

The beauty of service guidelines is that they allow everyone to bring something different to the table and contribute in their own way. Going above and beyond may temporarily take employees outside of their comfort zone, but so long as the process remains organic and feels like an extension of themselves, they'll continue to do so until their actions become second nature.

CREATING YOUR OWN

It's easy when you follow the Golden Rule: *Extend others the same respect and courtesy you would want in return.* Outstanding customer service begins with friendly gestures and answers to common questions then dazzling them with the VIP treatment. Here are some practical ways to treat your customers right:

Be Friendly

Communicate with direct eye contact and a warm smile to make others feel welcome.

Maintain Positive Body Language and Tone

Positive body language and tone exhibit professionalism and self-confidence. This includes proper posture, an attentive appearance, maintaining poise under pressure, the use of appropriate gestures, and respectful language.

Greet and Thank Every Customer

It's the customer who pays your salary, so extend a personalized warm welcome or thank you at the beginning and end of every transaction. Remember who regular customers are, and use their names or professional designations whenever possible.

Engage Customers

Take the initiative by reaching out to customers in need of assistance. Offer your undivided attention, ask questions, listen intently and solve their problems.

Be Helpful

Always take care of the customer with a *Yes We Can* approach. If something is unclear or you're unable to provide further assistance, promptly find somebody else who can.

Show, Don't Tell

Don't assume the customer knows where to go or that your instructions are clear. Physically escort them a reasonable distance to their point of interest whenever possible.

Offer the Right of Way

Be mindful of the customer and offer them the right of way when crossing paths.

Solicit Feedback

The best way to gain customer insight is to ask. Soliciting feedback opens the door for a conversation and ensures the customer's needs have been met.

As always, the goal is to strike the right balance between simplicity and clarity. Keeping your guidelines short and sweet looks good on paper, but you run the risk of leaving too much up for interpretation. Likewise, long-winded paragraphs are too confusing and rigid for customized service.

Once you've come up with your service guidelines, solicit feedback from your A-Team and make adjustments as required. The overall theme you want to communicate is that everything speaks to the customer and everyone's contributions come together to form the total package.

From here you're ready to put them into action. Like everything else we've done thus far, incorporate them into various training materials, link them to your vision and most importantly, practice what you preach!

* * *

Congratulations, you've just reached your first milestone and accomplished one of the most difficult parts of the program! Now that you've established the foundation for your company, the same must be done for your clone. The remaining chapters of this section will focus on creating new job descriptions for both of you, along with your respective leadership brands. From there we'll move on to Section Three and begin the actual cloning process.

Chapter 16

JOB DESCRIPTIONS

Job descriptions are used by most businesses these days and with good reason. They outline the qualifications, duties, and expectations for each position, and it's this transparency that enables the company to attract the right people from the get-go. Furthermore, job descriptions pave the way for a more comprehensive training program and a benchmark for the employee's performance.

Many entrepreneurs toil with bottleneck leadership because they haven't taken the time to define their own role. They see voids within the business and instinctively pick up the slack, instead of redirecting traffic to protect their time. Without a job description, there are no defined boundaries or areas of jurisdiction, and the leader can easily become sidetracked with other people's work. Therefore, it's critical to formalize the duties for both you and your clone, otherwise, you'll both be flying blind and condemned to the same fate.

In this chapter, we're going to create three job descriptions:

- o   One for your existing job, based on everything you're doing now

- o   A second for your dream job, based on your interests and goals

- o   A third for your clone, based on the requirements of the organization

Once complete, you'll have a firm understanding of where you are now, where you want to be, and how to get there. Similarly, the responsibilities of your clone will be carved in stone so there's no question what everyone must do.

YOUR EXISTING JOB DESCRIPTION

The first job description lists everything you're doing now, regardless of whether it's your responsibility or not. Your objective is to get everything on the table so you can decide which tasks you intend to keep, and which ones will be given to your clone.

Step 1: Make a List

Imagine it's Monday morning, and you have just arrived at work. What does your typical routine look like? What do you always do, where do you go and who do you speak with? Write down every responsibility you can think of and categorize them into daily, weekly, and monthly duties.

Your list should be comprised of specific, non-redundant tasks which can be directly measured. In other words, ignore things like problem-solving, delegating, and communicating, since these are processes not actual tasks.

To gain further insight into your position, consider the following questions:

- What purpose do I serve?
- Who depends on me and why?
- What problems do I solve?
- What does the company need from me?

Step 2: Journal Your Activities

In Chapter 3 we discussed the benefits of time journaling and how it can help determine exactly when and where your time is consumed. It's recommended to journal your activities for a few days to uncover anything you may have missed in the first step, as well as identifying the reoccurring disruptions in your day.

Step 3: Determine Qualifications and Skills

With a comprehensive list of duties in hand, you can now determine any specific qualifications and skills needed to perform the work.

Qualifications are mandatory technical or legal credentials required to do the job, such as First-Aid certification, a post-secondary degree, or number of years of experience.

Skills are favorable abilities or personal attributes to perform the job well, such as software proficiency, multilingualism, and strong problem-solving abilities.

Be sure to keep these lists separate because one outlines the prerequisites for the job, while the other merely describes what the ideal candidate looks like.

Step 4: Determine Training Requirements

Next, write down any specific training courses the company will facilitate, including: orientation, training videos, webinars, online courses and one-on-one training. Prioritize them based on importance and in conjunction with any third-party training which takes place.

Step 5: Pull It Together

You're now ready to start writing your job description, which typically follows the general format:

- o   Job Title and Department
- o   Reporting Structure (who supervises this role, if applicable)
- o   Position Summary
- o   Qualifications and Skills
- o   Training Requirements
- o   Responsibilities (duties organized chronologically into daily, weekly, monthly routines)

TIME-WIZARD TIP!

Save yourself the hassle and download this template at www.jeffhilderman.com/resources

Good Ideas:

- o Focus on tasks, not targets. Job descriptions shouldn't include performance standards

- o Group like responsibilities together to avoid redundancy

- o Avoid technical jargon, wordiness, and exaggerations

- o Focus on the company's requirements. Job descriptions shouldn't be constructed around an individual's personality, interests or experience

YOUR DREAM JOB DESCRIPTION

And now for the fun part! This is where you get to throw every obligation out the window and put the spotlight on you. What are your personal interests and aspirations? In which areas of the business would you like to explore new opportunities, and which duties would you happily hand off to your clone and never look back? What does the perfect work day look like for you? Dream big and write a job description for your future self.

Step 1: Look Back

Take a moment to reflect back on the original vision you had for yourself and your business. What were your dreams and what were you passionate about? This step is about rediscovering what drives you, what's fun and exciting– why you do what you do.

Are you a creative person who loves to innovate, design and build? Do you enjoy collaborating, networking and developing relationships? Maybe it's as simple as appreciating a good challenge and the satisfaction that comes with solving problems. There's no wrong answer, just write down whatever makes you happy and leaves you with a sense of accomplishment.

Step 2: Look Forward

Remove the shackles and drop everything that feels like a burden. If you had zero responsibilities when you arrived at work tomorrow, what would you do? What projects would you finally have time to work on? Maybe there's something you're doing now but just haven't had the opportunity to commit to wholeheartedly.

It can be something very specific like developing a new product or service, or something generic such as having more time to mingle with customers and interact with your team. Come up with your ultimate wish list, no matter how extravagant. You can also draw inspiration from your company's vision statement to imagine what the future looks like.

Step 3: List Your New Duties

Unfortunately, a dream job still has responsibilities, but at least these are ones you'll enjoy doing. Think about the action required to turn your aspirations into reality and create a set of duties for your new role. If there's anything in your existing job description that still interests you or requires your attention, like the financial side of the business, then this should also be included in your list.

Be very selective of your present tasks, choosing only the items you enjoy and absolutely have to do. Remember, the only way to make time for your new duties is to let many of your existing ones go.

Step 4: Create Your Job Description

Once again pull everything together and use the same guidelines to write a job description for your new role.

Step 5: Put It On Display

The final and most rewarding step is to post your new job description someplace where it will continuously encourage you to keep pushing forward. There will be ups and downs along the way, but know that there are blue skies ahead so embrace the change and own it!

YOUR CLONE'S JOB DESCRIPTION

Now that we've laid the groundwork to define the organization, your present role and the one you wish to pursue, we're finally ready to bring your clone into the conversation. This process will help identify who your ideal clone will be, the functions they'll perform and the necessary training required to make the transition as smooth as possible.

Step 1: Choose the Right Type of Clone

If you immediately stepped out of your current position and into the new one, what sort of void would your clone have to fill? Theoretically, the leftover duties from your existing job description would become your clone's responsibilities, but there are other points you'll need to think about:

- Are there any tasks that shouldn't be given to my clone and delegated elsewhere?

- Are there additional tasks I'm not presently doing that my clone should assume?

- Will my clone report directly to me, and if so, how will my absence affect them?

- Beyond the training period, how close will my clone and I work together every day?

Your answers will determine the type of clone you need. For example, if you intend on remaining at the helm of the company, your clone simply needs to think and act like you to assume the delegated responsibilities. But if you're planning on stepping out of the limelight altogether and contribute in a different capacity, your clone will step into a greater leadership role and inherit your authority as well.

Step 2: Finalize Duties

Draft a formalized set of duties for your clone based on everything we discussed in the previous step. Your list should resemble the same content and format as your existing job description.

Step 3: Create Their Job Description

For the third and final time, create a job description for your clone following the same instructions as before. You may want to consider a new job title, department, reporting structure and position summary depending on how your clone's role will differ from your own.

Step 4: Double Down on Training

What we haven't considered yet is who your clone will actually be. While an existing employee is the most logical choice because they're already familiar with the business, there are no guarantees this will be the case. To err on the side of caution, let's assume this person has no prior knowledge or experience about the company. Therefore, include the appropriate training to bring your clone up to speed on the organization's culture and how to preserve it.

That's it for job descriptions! Let's now shift gears to your leadership brand.

Chapter 17

YOUR LEADERSHIP BRAND

Everyone has a personal brand, even if they don't know it. For example, imagine a well-dressed man walks into a cafe at 6:00 am wearing an expensive suit, polished shoes, and a gold watch. He orders a coffee, sits down and begins to read the newspaper. What are your first impressions about this person? Would you say:

o   He carries himself well and takes pride in his appearance

o   He's successful because he can afford expensive clothing

o   His success is attributed to being an early riser and staying informed

It's judgmental, but also a fair assessment. So how does your perspective change, if the man:

o   Is friendly and faithfully tips the barista

o   Is rude and complains about the service

o   Arrived by bike instead of a car

o   Reeks of booze

o   Is reading the *Help Wanted* ads.

Interesting, isn't it? Our impression changes with each scenario, illustrating how our brain processes information. We take what we know and do our best to put two and two together. Maybe we're right, and maybe we're wrong, but until we receive more information, this is our perceived truth.

If the man drops a ten-dollar bill in the tip jar every day, it's assumed he will do this again upon his next visit. Likewise, if the man is always a belligerent jerk, the staff will instantly be on guard every time he walks through the doors.

Our appearance, attitude, and behavior all contribute to our reputation which, good or bad, will eventually precede our presence. However, left unchecked this could result in discrepancies between our self-image and others' perceptions, leading to misunderstandings, damaged relationships and a disconnect with reality.

For instance, the rude man could actually be an all-around nice guy – he's just not a morning person and likes his coffee a particular way. In fact, he could be completely oblivious to his negative projection and how he portrays himself to everyone else. Pretty scary when you think about it.

So when it comes to our personal brand, we have two options: we can either do nothing and let others misjudge us from a distance, or alternatively, we can take control, and cultivate our personal brand by consciously carrying ourselves in the manner we wish to be seen.

YOUR LEADERSHIP BRAND

When you were first discovering yourself as a leader, things probably felt awkward to no end. I'm sure there were missteps along the way (I certainly had my fair share), but eventually you found your footing and became a proficient leader. During this time, you've developed your trademark style of getting things done– this is your leadership brand.

Right now, everyone knows what they can expect from you and what you expect in return. Your brand conveys your talents as a leader, a critical component to gaining the respect of your team and influencing their behavior. But this begs the question: is your leadership brand the right one for you and your business? Let's review the essential building blocks of a leadership brand and put yours to the test.

THE BUILDING BLOCKS

Creating an authentic and reputable brand doesn't happen over night, nor does it have a check box beside it. The process is constantly evolving as you adapt your own style and abilities as a leader to meet the demands of the company. A well-established brand can take years to temper, and even then it must be managed with diligence.

The outcome is two-fold, the first ensuring your self-image coincides with the perception others have of you. This requires careful planning and execution on your part to create a leadership brand which is authentically you. Secondly and most importantly, your brand must consistently deliver the goods. There are numerous expectations placed on you by your customers, employees, and partners, and their faith in you is directly related to the results you produce.

Authenticity

People want to follow real companies with real leaders, those who are relatable and share similar beliefs. Creating an authentic leadership brand means defining the type of leader you will be and how others will connect with you. They can spot a fake a mile away so avoid marketing yourself in any way that's misleading, and confirm your vision and values are aligned with the organization's culture. If you have the courage to be yourself and lead with your heart, others will be inspired to do the same.

Deliverability

The very essence of a leadership brand is to showcase your personal proficiency, demonstrating your ability to exercise sound judgment, promote teamwork, develop talent, execute plans, and deliver results. Great leaders understand that trust, respect, and loyalty are earned the old-fashioned way, by following through on your promises and leading by example. Deliverability is about being the leader everyone depends on you to be.

Consistency

Your employees are like children, each with specific needs who push their boundaries to see how you react. They might be testing the waters to determine what they can get away with, or perhaps they need the reassurance of a safety net before venturing out on their own. Either way, they're impressionable and always watching you!

So what message are you sending if your leadership style sways in the wind? How can you hold others accountable when you're not modeling the correct behavior yourself? Consistency is what allows your brand to take root, but this means being an exemplary role model and mindful of your actions at all times.

Growth

With the intense focus you place on your customers and employees, it's easy to lose sight of your own needs – especially when it comes to personal development. Even the most seasoned leaders regularly hone their skills and look for ways to broaden their capabilities, so they can stay ahead of the curve.

Your leadership brand should embrace growth as much as it does to promote it in others. Be open-minded, ask questions and listen intently to further your understanding instead of being dismissive. Set goals, learn from mistakes, and foster an environment that rewards innovation over preserving the status quo.

HOW TO CULTIVATE YOUR BRAND

Step 1: Describe Your Future Self

Write down 8-12 words that best describe you, your values and strengths. How do you hope to be identified as a leader?

Step 2: Describe the Necessary Behavior

Determine what action must be taken to realize your brand, in terms of:

- o   Your appearance, body language, attitude, and energy

- o   How you will articulate yourself and communicate with others

- o   Your commitment to building teams and developing individuals

- o   Your creative contributions and overall presence

Step 3: Formalize Your Brand

Write a mission statement for yourself to make it official. What's your purpose and call to action?

Step 4: Set Yourself Up for Success

Create a daily routine to support the new desired behavior. Post your mission statement in a visible location and set reminders for yourself to keep your actions in check. Continue this process until your actions become habits.

Step 5: Quietly Live Your Brand

Any proclamations of your new identity and agenda will be received as either a fad or an identity crisis. Actions speak louder than words, so quietly live your brand and let others discover it for themselves.

Your leadership brand plays a pivotal role when it comes to training and developing your clone. Take a moment to review your brand in conjunction with the job descriptions you created earlier. Are your present behaviors aligned with your future expectations? Are you the best version of yourself you'd like to clone? If the answers are no, then it's time to put your money where your mouth is and start living the part to a tee.

* * *

Holy cow, you did it! Hopefully, this marks the end of your first thirty days, but if it took a little longer, don't sweat it. What matters is that you've accomplished a huge undertaking in a short period of time, and the most intense part of the program is now behind you.

You've formalized your belief system and established the company's foundation. For the first time, you have a clear understanding of who you are, where you want to be, and how you'll get there. The blueprint is complete, and now it's time to take action.

Let's continue to Section Three, where we'll kick off another thirty-day stint and cover everything related to finding and training your clone.

Section Three

DEVELOPING YOUR CLONE

Chapter 18

FINDING YOUR CLONE

Passing the torch is one of the most nerve-racking challenges every leader will face during their career. The exchange of responsibility and authority is far from symbolic, given that the future of the organization and its members relies on a smooth transition. Likewise, the corresponding pressure placed on the successor is tremendous, as is the leader's undertaking to choose the right person to carry on their legacy.

Great employees are tough to find, even with a steady flow of candidates on your doorstep. Some people are truly passionate about hiring and excel at what they do, but for the rest of us it's a tedious experience. Unfortunately, with this mindset, we treat the hiring process as a monotonous task instead of an opportunity to increase the company's diversity and caliber of talent. Consequently, the goal becomes to fill the position out of convenience rather than finding the ideal fit for the role.

Truth be told, I didn't find my clone right out of the gate. I took a shortcut by hiring a glorified assistant who would be easy to train, despite having the wrong personality to eventually lead in my stead. I chose convenience over quality, and it bit me in the butt six months later when things didn't work out.

While this certainly shouldn't be condoned as regular hiring practices, the truth is, that a reasonably healthy culture can endure a few duds. The employee may or may not work out, but the company will continue to chug along regardless of the outcome.

However, the same can't be said for those in a position of authority who can change the company's direction and alter the organization's culture. As the stakes become much higher, the process and decision to find the qualified person must not be taken lightly. After all, history has proven time and time again that no organization is immune from faulty leadership.

Choosing your clone will be one of the most important decisions you make, but this doesn't mean it needs to be difficult. It just comes down to understanding your options and placing your attention on the right things to ensure your clone's personality, and leadership style is compatible with your own.

GO OUTSIDE OR LOOK WITHIN

When it comes to hiring, it's not always clear whether to open the floodgates or go with who you know. Most would agree an internal promotion is the preferred choice, considering the person is already familiar with the company's operations and has a rapport with the team. It's usually faster and less expensive to bring them up to speed than it would be with an outside hire, not to mention it sends a strong message to everyone else hopeful for future growth opportunities.

But hiring from within may not always be the most viable solution, especially if the company needs an injection of energy, new skills or creative perspectives. People who have thrived in different industries tend to possess transferable skill sets such as delegation and team development, and can even shed new light on how operations and logistics could be improved.

Although there isn't a one-size-fits-all approach when it comes to finding your clone, there are general guidelines that can aid in the selection process:

Promote internally, if:

- ✓ The organization's culture is healthy
- ✓ The candidate is a natural fit for the role and can be taught the necessary skills
- ✓ The rest of the team would support the candidate

Hire externally, if:

- ✓ The organization's culture is unhealthy

- ✓ The company lacks eligible candidates

- ✓ An internal promotion would disrupt the team's cohesiveness and camaraderie

- ✓ Sufficient training resources are available to recruit and integrate the candidate

There are pros and cons either way you slice it, so the real determining factor is how well they'll fit into and preserve the organization's culture. Having the right person at the helm will safeguard the company's vision and longevity, while the wrong person can quickly break down all that has been accomplished.

CHOOSING THE RIGHT NEEDLE IN THE HAYSTACK

Nobody is the perfect fit, regardless of how impressive their credentials are. The priority should be set on finding the person most likely to embrace the company's culture, assimilate into the team and deliver great customer service, over those who have multiple degrees and a long list of references.

The same can be said about matching the right personality for the intended role. An introvert, who by nature keeps to themselves, may excel in their current position because their work demands minimal contact with others. However, promoting them into a leadership role could present serious challenges if they're uncomfortable with confrontation and being sought out for guidance. But that doesn't automatically make extroverts the better choice, given their outgoing personality could come off as too assertive and may rub people the wrong way.

The point is that there isn't a specific needle you're looking for in the haystack. Everyone comes with their own set of experience, ambitions, strengths, and flaws, and it's your job to evaluate the total package to determine who's most likely to assume your duties and be followed by the team. To identify the person who will best serve as your clone, examine each candidate through the same lens using the following criteria:

Assess Their Values

Arguably the most important step is to assess their core values and evaluate their compatibility to the organizational culture. An exact match isn't necessary, but they do have to resonate the same underlying theme and convince you that their decisions and behaviors will closely resemble your own. Your team's effectiveness, along with the company's productivity and efficiency, all hinge on consistent leadership before, during and after the transfer of duties.

Recruit an A-Team Player

Don't settle for anything less than a top performer. It's not about who's been around the longest or *deserves* it out of circumstance, this person must earn the part by proving they can think, walk and talk just as quickly as you do. I'm talking about the positive, high energy, self-motivating types who excel in both individual and team environments. The ones who channel their energy into building others up and doing the right thing without concern for who gets the credit.

Teaching your clone the necessary skills to do the job is one thing, but babysitting them over the fundamentals is another. All candidates should already be proficient with nearly everything we discussed in Section One, otherwise, you're just setting both of you up for failure.

The best employee you have is you, which means your clone must be your number two.

Gage Their Emotional and Mental Fortitude

Nobody leads without facing criticism and discouragement, but then again, nobody truly leads without pushing through it as well. Your clone will face the same anxiety as you to make tough decisions, solve problems under pressure and continuously adapt to change.

Walk them through real-life situations you've encountered and role-play with them as they try to work through the situation. Throw unexpected (but reasonable) curve balls at them on the spot to understand their thought process and gage how well they react under pressure. In times of adversity, the team will turn to your clone for guidance, so it's imperative they demonstrate emotional intelligence and remain logical to get the job done.

Pay Attention to How They Communicate

The ability to clearly articulate direction and provide feedback is a prerequisite for any leader, but the manner in which they speak will show you who they really are. How confident do they sound and are they charismatic enough to rouse the troops when needed? Do you get the impression they might be too soft or firm relatives to your own leadership style? How do they speak of previous colleagues; are they respectful and hold them in high regard, or do they finger-point and deflect responsibility? Be mindful of their answers, and read between the lines to evaluate if their personality and style are what you're looking for in a clone.

Get an Upgradable Version

As the business grows and your interests change, you'll eventually want to hand more responsibilities over to your clone. A final point of consideration is how proficient your clone would be at running the business side of the business – all the financial stuff that's usually the last part to be let go by the leader.

This includes financial forecasting, understanding revenue streams, managing expenses, analyzing inventory, overseeing marketing campaigns, and strategizing future growth. While this may not be an immediate concern right now, you'll want to be sure you're investing in the right person that can assume the remainder of your responsibilities and act as your true clone instead of as a glorified manager.

CHECK IT OUT!

You can download your own checklist, along with my Top Ten Interview Questions at www.jeffhilderman.com/resources

DON'T RUSH IT

Finding your clone might sound like a relatively straightforward process, but the truth is you may have to conduct several rounds of interviews to find the right person for the job. It's very tempting to just go with somebody who's already in front of you, but if your gut is telling you to keep on looking, take your own advice! You're always better off pushing your plans back a week or two instead of rushing in, only to find yourself back where you started a year from now.

As a final disclaimer, remember, it's just as easy to hold out for the perfect catch who will never come along. As I mentioned earlier, you only want to recruit A-team players, but this doesn't mean you hold everyone to impossible standards either.

What it really comes down to is your confidence that they'll be a natural fit into the organization and can learn the skills needed to perform their job. If you still haven't found somebody in a month's time, you may need to go back to the drawing board and re-evaluate your hiring strategies and conditions.

Chapter 19

TRAINING YOUR CLONE

Everybody wins when employee training is embedded into the organization's culture as a top priority. New employees are welcomed with open arms and equipped with the knowledge and skills needed to succeed in their new role. Long-term employees are committed to supporting them in every capacity, and even seize the opportunity to brush up on their own skills, so they can continue to meet the demands of an ever-changing landscape. And as a whole, the business reaps the rewards of an energized, efficient workforce, ready and willing to carry out the company's mission.

But none of this happens by accident, and it requires a company-wide initiative to make it successful. When a lukewarm approach is taken to employee development, it naturally leaves the door open for inconsistent practices and serious consequences that go beyond the new hire. Once again, this was a lesson I had to learn the hard way.

In 2006, I stepped into a mid-level managerial role directly overseeing the daily operations of six departments. My team was comprised of four supervisors and another thirty employees with varying responsibilities and experience. This was also at a time when our local economy was leading the country's economic growth rate and had an unemployment rate of 3%, half the national average[7]. Our market was white hot, which was great for business, but made it nearly impossible to find qualified help.

To give you a sense of how difficult it was to find anyone, billboards lined the streets advertising ridiculous offers like a $5000 signing bonus for a short-order cook. Inexperienced cashiers could easily find a job paying $16/hour (minimum

---

[7] "Unemployment Rates in Alberta and Canada," Statistics Canada. www.statcan.gc.ca/daily-quotidien/160205/cg-a003-eng.htm.

wage was less than $10), while truck drivers made in upwards of $80. It was a human resources' nightmare, so needless to say, when you had a half-decent candidate apply for a job, you held on to them for dear life.

Such was the case with a young lady who was hired as a sales associate. Ally didn't have much experience, but she was a firecracker. She had a permanent smile on her face, endless energy, and did whatever was asked of her without hesitation. She was the definition of a team player and a godsend at a time when we were struggling to keep our heads above water. We hit the jackpot, and then we screwed it up.

In the beginning, we went through the motions of our typical training program. She was given an orientation, introduced to her team, and equipped with the basic knowledge for her to do her job. Her willingness to please was a breath of fresh air and something her supervisor latched on to right away. She was great with customers, and despite her lack of knowledge, did what she could and put forth her best effort every time.

Sadly, eighteen months later, Ally wasn't the same person we had hired. Her training had taken a backseat to daily to-do lists, and it showed. Ally's smile no longer felt genuine, she made all sorts of costly mistakes and upset many customers along the way. She lacked the confidence and ambition to continue her job, and it wasn't her fault. Her supervisor failed her when he no longer placed her needs ahead of his own, and I failed both of them doing the exact same thing.

Ally left shortly after that, and it was a devastating loss. I tried everything to keep her on board, but it was futile, and to be honest, I couldn't blame her. Even worse, we lost her supervisor later that year and dealt with the fallout for months after his departure. There were all sorts of problems, expensive mistakes, and upset customers, never mind everything involved in replacing both of the people we had lost.

I blamed myself and swore I'd never let this happen again. From now on, employee development would always be treated as a top priority. We owed it to everyone on our team, and especially to the ones we had let slip through our fingers.

So what's the lesson from this cautionary tale? Failure to identify and reconcile problems early on will eventually lead to a domino effect of broken down communication, efficiency, and team morale, which can tarnish the company's reputation – and its bottom line.

It's an unfortunate situation when the company loses a good person to bad training, but it can be even more disastrous if they stay on board.

THE RIGHT WAY TO TRAIN

We previously discussed the three stages of cultural implementation and the respective changes that must occur. The same model can be used to create a systematic training program which balances the expectations of the company with the learning requirements of the employee.

The Three Fundamental Principles for an Effective Training Program can be rewritten as:

1. Change what is known, with instruction and practice

2. Change what is believed, with observation and feedback

3. Change what is habitual, with structure and accountability

Many leaders fail to understand or respect the process in which change must occur. They view training as merely an exchange of knowledge, when in fact, this portion is minimal compared to the time and energy invested in reinforcing the correct behavior until they become habits.

I often see employee training treated like a marketing campaign on steroids, with an intense focus over a short period of time that eventually fizzles out. Facilitators, who are eager to get *through* the material rather than *into* the material, make the mistake of cramming too much into training sessions, rendering them largely ineffective. Without the necessary opportunities to seek clarification, digest the content, and put it into practice, recruits typically fall victim to information overload and are then accused of not catching on quickly enough.

While there are no certainties in how well an employee will perform or how long they'll stick around. What is known, is that the quality of your training program will have a direct bearing on the result. With the right formula and a firm commitment to employee development, your business will flourish with top performers and remain both competitive and profitable for years to come.

BASIC TRAINING

The importance of structure within a company's training program can't be overstated. This framework, which includes a formalized itinerary, quality content, defined learning objectives, strategies, and delivery systems, establishes a standard for consistent training which can be easily measured and enforced. In doing so, everyone's needs will be accommodated, and you can rest easy knowing your newest prospects are in good hands.

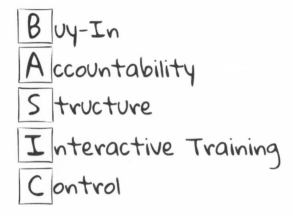

B uy-In
A ccountability
S tructure
I nteractive Training
C ontrol

The BASIC Training Model is everything you need to bring your clone (or anyone else) up to speed, regardless of their previous experience. It's the foundation for your entire training program now and moving forward, and can be customized to your heart's content as your business continues to evolve. BASIC Training consists of the following components:

Buy-In

Most experts would agree that creating buy-in is the most critical component of any training program. From the very first day, employees should embrace the organizational culture and have a clear understanding of how their contributions fit into the bigger picture.

Additionally, this is where your clone's leadership brand should be discussed in relation to your own. The onboarding process should be fun and exciting to ward off any nerves that come with starting a new job, which in turn, sets the tone for a safe and encouraging learning environment.

Accountability

The next step is to communicate everything your clone will be held accountable for and how their performance will be benchmarked against the company's expectations. This includes the duties, skills, and qualifications outlined in their job description, as well as any financial goals, marketing initiatives, and standards that must be upheld.

Your clone may also need clarification of the organizational hierarchy and the details surrounding their jurisdiction to effectively do their job. Establishing accountability early on will enable you to measure their progress and open the door for any constructive feedback.

Structure

You've thrown all the cards on the table, so now it's time to come up with a plan. Creating bite-size learning objectives, accompanied with their respective deadlines, will help keep everyone on schedule and make the entire process seem less daunting.

Similarly, incorporating their normal duties into a daily routine will create the structure needed to consistently model the right behavior. All of this will be reviewed with your clone ahead of time and treated as mutually-shared goals, rather than an intimidating to-do list, so they understand the process and, hopefully, feel more comfortable with the work that lies ahead.

Interactive Training

Keep the handbooks in the drawer for this one, or at the very least, minimize their use. The purpose of interactive training is to employ various learning tactics, so recruits stay interested and receptive.

Instead of rambling on about policies, tell engaging stories about great service and overcoming challenges. Determine where it would be appropriate to use videos, online training, and job-shadowing. Encourage them to roll up their sleeves and learn by making mistakes, all while, building their confidence and focusing on the things they're doing right. Who says training can't be educational *and* fun!

Control

Your clone must be empowered to make decisions on their own, solve problems, voice opinions, assist one another and uphold company standards. It's about extending trust and getting out of the way so they can do their job.

It's your responsibility to mentor them on improving what's already been done, not shield them from failure or figure it out on their behalf. Your success came from learning hard lessons and discovering your own leadership style, and if you expect your clone to follow in your footsteps, they must be given the freedom to walk a similar path.

The BASIC Training Model defines the fundamental components of employee training and the sequential order in which the program should be carried out. Now that we've established the general layout, we can begin adding the content to create an itinerary for your clone.

Chapter 20

THE EMPLOYEE RECORD

Now that you're familiar with the elements of BASIC Training, we can apply these principles to create a specialized itinerary, known as an Employee Record, to make your clone's first week an absolute success. Each day is carefully constructed around specific learning objectives and delivery systems, such as videos, job-shadowing, hands-on training, and personal discussion.

As your clone progresses through the week, they'll become more comfortable with the training process, along with the duties they've incorporated into their daily routine.

To clarify, this is different from the job description you created earlier. While job descriptions are an essential training tool, they do not establish:

X   Employee buy-in

X   Various learning methods

X   Regular points of communication and feedback

X   Goals and accountability

Think of a job description like a book's table of contents and the Employee Record is the first chapter. The table of contents is a convenient reference tool and helps determine whether or not the book is for you, but ultimately, it's the first chapter that sets the tone and captures your interest.

Similarly, your clone's first week on the job represents the first chapter of their new story, and without structure, they're highly susceptible to becoming overwhelmed, undertrained, and out of sync with the organization's culture.

So, in summary, the **Employee Record supplements the job description to create a structured learning environment that's conducive to employee engagement and the development of proper habits**, ensuring all the BASIC Training criteria is met. This way, your clone will have a comprehensive list of everything that's expected of them, including an action plan that sends the message you're committed to their personal development.

Employee Record

Name: _____   Date: _____

Department: _____   Full Time   Part Time

Position: _____   Permanent   Seasonal

Employee Number: _____   Supervisor: _____

Day 1

☐ Administrative Check-In   ☐ Tours & Introductions   ☐ Schedule

☐ Orientation Presentation   ☐ Safety Training   ☐ Feedback

Day 2

☐ Orientation Video 1   ☐ Review Job Description   ☐ Job Shadow

☐ Introduction to Dept.   ☐ Equipment Training   ☐ Feedback

Day 3

☐ Orientation Video 2   ☐ Review Daily Routine   ☐ Free Time

☐ Job Shadow (AM)   ☐ Review Top 5 Policies   ☐ Feedback

Day 4

☐ Orientation Video 3   ☐ Equipment Inspections   ☐ Job Shadow

☐ Online Training   ☐ Hands On Training   ☐ Feedback

Day 5

☐ Daily Routine   ☐ Online Training 2   ☐ Week in Review

☐ Review Weekly Routine   ☐ Safety Review   ☐ Feedback

This is an example of what your Employee Record could look like. Take note that the generic items listed here are merely to illustrate the use of different delivery systems, and in reality, you'd want to be as specific as possible.

TIME-WIZARD TIP!

Save yourself the hassle and download this template at www.jeffhilderman.com/resources

CREATING YOUR OWN

With your clone's job description beside you, we can now utilize the BASIC Training Model to create their employee record.

Step 1: Create an Outline

Begin by laying out the general format for the Employee Record. This will include an area for any relevant employee information and a distinct header for each day of the week. New employees will need to check in with Administration prior to training; so this can be listed as the first item on Day 1, along with any other housekeeping tasks:

- Complete administrative paperwork such as personal information and confidentially agreements
- Distribute uniform, stationery supplies, equipment, and schedule
- Take photo and setup ID cards, passwords, etc.
- Demonstrate use of time clock and issue a locker or workstation

Depending on the nature of your business, you may also want to conduct safety training on the first day so both of you can hit the ground running on day two.

Step 2: Generate Buy-In

The first week of training is when your clone is most impressionable to understand and embrace the organization's culture. Creating buy-in should begin immediately with an onboarding presentation on their first day, where they're introduced to the company's vision, mission, and values. Not only will this build anticipation for their new job, but it will also plant the seeds for everything else they're about to learn and experience. After the initial presentation, orientation continues with a tour and team introductions.

Of course, all of this novelty buzz will eventually wear off, so creating long-term buy-in is where the real work begins. Continuous reinforcement must be interwoven in layers using a variety of methods, such as training materials, job-shadowing, and personalized coaching. Even something as simple as reiterating the company mantra during informal feedback sessions can pack a serious punch.

Write down all the ways you can engage your clone and work them into each day's agenda. Remember that creating buy-in is an ongoing process, so be sure to adapt your own routine so you can maintain the momentum in the following weeks and months to come.

Step 3: Communicate Accountability

As tempting as it may be to jump right into your clone's responsibilities on their first day, don't do it! The plan is to reserve day one exclusively for check-in procedures and buy-in strategies to keep their attention focus on the organization's culture. This way your core message won't be diluted, and there will be adequate time for your clone to process everything they've absorbed. You'll find that taking the slow-and-steady approach on day one will dramatically increase their receptiveness, level of engagement, and ability to subconsciously link their behaviors to core company values.

The primary objective of day two is to paint a picture of your clone's future. You'll still want to break up the day with onboarding sessions and hands-on experience, but this is the time to sit down with your clone and outline everything that's expected of them. Set aside a couple of hours to review their job description with them, highlighting the key duties that will encompass their daily, weekly, and monthly routines.

This is also the appropriate time to touch on any performance standards, service guidelines, financial and marketing directives that will affect their position. At this point, don't get too hung up on specifics, the intent is to unveil the bigger picture without bombarding them with information.

Step 4: Establish Structure

Setting goals and routines is a two-step process. First is the planning phase, where you'll use their job description as a guide to create an itinerary for the remainder of the week. Careful consideration must be taken to avoid cramming too much into a single day. The *sink or swim* approach is an outdated philosophy, as it only promotes anxiety and rushes the learning process. Instead, think of training like building a tower, where each day is dedicated to adding another block and securing it in place.

Review your clone's job description and come up with an essential Top Ten List comprised of policies, procedures, and physical training. This list should represent the core functions of their position and be arranged in a manner that closely follows their daily routine. Insert these training sessions into the next three days, and if possible, structure each morning or afternoon around the central theme of the day's buy-in message. Again, the purpose is to connect the dots between actions and values, which we know is a prerequisite to forming the right habits.

Once you're satisfied with the content and general layout of the Employee Record, the second step is to incorporate this into the accountability conversation you'll have with your clone on day two. This will make up the second half of your discussion, which will address how they'll be trained and what they can expect – providing a broader scope of their future.

So in reality, your accountability conversation will look something like this:

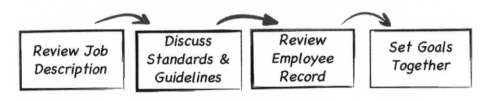

Review Job Description → Discuss Standards & Guidelines → Review Employee Record → Set Goals Together

While your clone is technically agreeing to the itinerary you've presented them, the conversation will naturally flow from points A to B and feel more like a mutually-shared plan. The benefit of using this approach is two-fold, as it will:

1. Establish accountability at the very beginning of the training process

2. Create an environment where trust and rapport can develop over time.

Step 5: Incorporate Interactive Methods

There are no certainties when it comes to employee training, so field-testing various delivery systems in the first week will help identify what your clone is most receptive to. With a better understanding of their personality, learning preferences, and abilities, you can tailor your coaching style and training methods to better match the needs of your clone.

Determining which delivery system to use will depend on the type of learning taking place. First, we have **Verbal Delivery Systems**, which utilizes both dialog and written directives to convey information. For example, face-to-face conversations are best suited for employee engagement and buy-in because it humanizes the entire process. The message feels more *real* in person and can be influenced by tone, inflection, volume, and dramatic pauses to inspire action.

Company handbooks, lists, and forms all have their place in this category as well but should be seen more as referral tools for policies and procedures. Your clone won't remember everything, but knowing the information is within arm's reach will increase their confidence and reduce performance anxiety. Keep in mind, however, that your clone's preferred learning style may be conducive to reading before doing, which in this case should be encouraged and accommodated whenever possible.

A picture is worth a thousand words, and sometimes, it's just easier to see it rather than explain it. **Visual Delivery Systems** rely on images, colors and mind maps to impart information, which is ideal for organizing thoughts and breaking down larger systems into bite-sized pieces. Consider using diagrams as visual aids during orientation to reinforce what's being said. Flow charts and similar resources can also be used during job-shadowing sessions to instill confidence and train your clone to become self-reliant.

Lastly, there are **Physical Delivery Systems** which take a hands-on approach to learning. This system is perfect for teaching new skills in a controlled environment and how to maintain composure under pressure. Things won't always go as planned, so your clone must learn how to think on their feet and get used to being outside their comfort zone. Alternative training methods could include role playing scenarios, hands-on experimentation and encouraging safe mistakes.

So to quickly recap the three types of delivery systems:

- o   *Verbal* systems are ideal for creating buy-in and policy referral
- o   *Visual* systems are ideal for communicating big picture concepts
- o   *Physical* systems are ideal for practicing skills and contingencies

Of course, these are only guidelines, and in many cases, they can be used in different combinations to create a truly interactive experience. Review your clone's employee record and visualize how each training session would play out. Careful consideration should be taken to determine where the training will take place, by whom, and what resources are available with respect to the chosen delivery system.

Once you have the logistics figured out, rewrite the employee record to specify some details. For example, instead of generically listing job-shadowing, rewrite it as *Customer Service Training (JS)*. Replace *Review Top 5 Policies*, with *Coaching Session – Top 5 Policies*. The point isn't to rewrite everything for the sake of making it sound better, but instead, to clarify what that training session will entail.

As a final test, put yourself in your clone's shoes and imagine what their first five days would look like. Does it feel like you're steadily moving forward each day, and are the training sessions different enough to keep you on your toes? Are there ample opportunities to have face-to-face conversations and ask questions? Continue to review and revise each day until you are satisfied with the itinerary as a whole.

Step 6: Commissioning Your Clone

This will become more relevant at the actual time of training, but there's one last point worth mentioning. Training is similar to ballroom dancing in the sense that one person is always leading and the other is following. It will be your job to do all of the leading for the first few days, but afterward, your clone should be given opportunities to lead as well. The intent is to subtly challenge them to step out from under your wing and take ownership of their training. Doing so will enable them to secure their own victories and build the necessary confidence to be an effective leader.

Chapter 21

ORIENTATION

First impressions are everything in business. From polished resumes to polished shoes, top performers know they have a single opportunity to sell themselves as the best person for the job. But this goes both ways, and the organization should be just as concerned with making the right first impression in return. Orientation is an opportunity to calm nerves and reassure the employee they've made the right choice.

ORIENTATION VS. ONBOARDING

Before we go any further, let's quickly clarify the difference between orientation and onboarding. **Orientation** is the initial period of time in which an employee acclimatizes to their new role, team, and environment. It begins on their first day – typically comprised of paperwork, housekeeping tasks, and introductions – and continues throughout the week. The specific duration of the orientation will depend on the person and industry, but generally speaking, a week is sufficient to get settled in.

Onboarding is the umbrella term we use to describe an employee's cultural development and alignment. Earlier, when we discussed the procedure for cultural implementation, you'll recall the first step was to *change what was known by understanding the new way of doing things* – this is onboarding! It's about communicating your why and getting others *onboard* with your vision. But this isn't a one-shot deal, in fact, onboarding is an ongoing form of engagement that keeps the organization's health in check.

Ok, let's get down to business and create your orientation program.

PRE-ORIENTATION

Your new employee will probably feel anxious on their first day, and being unprepared for their arrival will only make things worse. A Pre-Orientation Checklist is useful for keeping everything (and everyone) on track leading up to the big day and will ensure the employee feels as comfortable as possible.

Your checklist should include the following items:

- o   Contact the employee and confirm their start date

- o   Send a welcome email including the details of where to go, who to report to and what to bring. Also, attach a copy of the company handbook to be read ahead of time

- o   Advise your team about the new hire, their position, and start date

- o   Prepare their workspace with the necessary equipment and supplies

- o   Setup their email, passwords, ID tags, parking, and locker assignments

- o   Prepare the necessary documents and verify they're up to date (administrative forms, training material, job description, employee record, etc.)

- o   Review the employee record with your team and plan out their first week

- o   Block off time on your calendar when you'll be directly involved with training

TIME-WIZARD TIP!

Save yourself the hassle and download this template at www.jeffhilderman.com/resources

ORIENTATION DAY

If you've done your due diligence with the Job Description, Employee Record, and Pre-Orientation Checklist, there's no reason why their first day shouldn't be smooth sailing. As per the employee record, the first order of business should be the administrative check-in, immediately followed by the onboarding presentation.

Let's not forget about your own first impression, beginning with your punctuality and demeanor. You should be notified immediately after the employee has begun their paperwork so you can wrap up what you're doing and prepare for the presentation. Keeping the employee waiting at any point is not only unprofessional and damaging to your brand, but it could also make it more difficult to create buy-in when talking about prompt service.

Another rule of thumb is to leave your emotional baggage at the door before introductions. It doesn't matter how busy you are or what problems you're dealing with, it's your job to stay cool and shield them from any potential stress. After a warm welcome, both of you can proceed to wherever the onboarding presentation will take place.

THE ONBOARDING PRESENTATION

This doesn't have be a high-tech PowerPoint display, but if that's your thing go for it! An informal meeting over a cup of coffee can be just as effective, but keep in mind the meeting should match the workplace. A business with a goofy, relaxed culture shouldn't misrepresent themselves with a corporate-themed orientation and vice versa.

The format is entirely up to you so long as the fundamental objectives are met:

- ✓ To minimize the employee's anxiety and reaffirm the company's commitment on training
- ✓ To communicate the Cultural Framework and generate buy-in
- ✓ To convince the employee their contributions matter and serve a higher purpose
- ✓ To reassure the employee the company is right for them

We won't go too deeply into the art of public speaking and presentation development since there are entire books dedicated to this subject, but here's a few tried-and-true tips to get you started.

Do Your Homework

This will be one of the most important conversations you ever have with your employee, so needless to say, shooting from the hip is ill-advised. There's a lot of work that goes into building a presentation, but with a polished copy of the company's vision, mission, and values, you're already half way there. All that remains is to link your thoughts together and tell a story that somebody on the outside would want to hear. Know your facts, be clear and keep it entertaining, that's all there is to it.

Use Real-Life Examples

Buy-in comes from building rapport and being relatable. Nobody wants to listen to theoretical situations or stories exaggerated for effect– this will only erode their patience and your credibility. What people really want to hear about is your own personal struggles, lessons, and triumphs. By exposing your human side (as opposed to your corporate brand), you become relatable. Only then will your authenticity shine through and others will be willing to trust what you have to say.

Remember, the onboarding process is all about making that emotional connection with the employee and linking their behaviors to specific values. If you want them to buy into the vision, you must be first willing to expose the real you and everything that comes with it.

Bring Them into the Conversation

It's your choice: either speak to capture their attention or discuss to capture their interest. Participation and engagement go hand in hand, because there's no joy being on the receiving end of a one-way conversation.

Direct participation occurs when others consciously agree to take part in an exercise, ideal for recapturing their attention and adding value to the conversation. For example, if you ask someone within a group to share a story or present a problem, everyone's attention will refocus on the new speaker. Even better, the solution or value you offer will reward the listeners for their undivided attention and keep them interested in whatever else you have to say.

Indirect participation, on the other hand, is a clever way to get others to participate without awareness– ideal for generating buy-in. You can help your audience form a mental picture by instructing them to *imagine, picture or visualize* whatever you're describing. If they can see it in their mind, they will better understand and believe what you're saying.

Another way to create buy-in is through subtle acknowledgment. Asking rhetorical questions such as "Does this make sense?" or "Is that clear?" after an important claim will be enough to induce head nodding and even a verbal response. When you see this going on, you'll know you have them exactly where you want them.

Start Strong, Finish Stronger

Predictable is boring, and boring is not memorable. You've only got sixty seconds to capture their attention before they start counting the ceiling tiles, so forego the lengthy introductions and jump right into a story. After you've hooked them in with your first talking point, you can always go back to formally introduce yourself and review the agenda.

Virtually every story follows the same arched structure, beginning with a problem that escalates in tension, eventually leading to the climax and resolution. While the same format can be used to share your own stories and antidotes, the overall structure of your presentation should more closely resemble a crescendo that only increases in intensity.

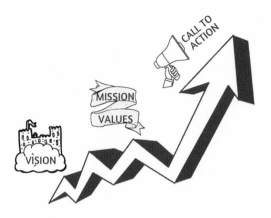

Begin by painting a picture of what your vision looks like and then expand on the details. Next, reveal the larger picture by including the organization's mission and company values, and then wrap things up with an inspirational message and call to action. To end on a high note, you'll need to keep your presentation under ninety minutes, so if it means trimming down stories and examples, do it!

Don't Blow It!

Practice, practice, practice! You've come this far, and the last thing you need is to fumble through your presentation and have your message fall on deaf ears. Rehearse your speech out loud until you can recite it in your sleep. Work on your delivery, choose your wording, time your pauses, and make sure the theatrics match the room.

If the onboarding presentation is just between you and your clone, minimize the awkwardness by remaining seated across from them and speak in a more casual tone. If, however, you're giving a speech to a group of people, by all means, stand up and own the room. Either way, keep the energy high and the dialog interactive.

If the employee has previous experience with the company and you're wondering if any of this is still applicable, the answer is yes! Even if they've heard some version of this presentation before, there are benefits to going through it again. Not only is it an opportunity to reinforce what they've learned and experienced in their former position, but they may also gain new insight into the bigger picture the second time around.

THE HANDOFF

If you've done your job correctly, the employee should be coming out of the presentation feeling energized and eager to work. The absolute wrong thing to do at this point is to kill the momentum by slamming them with a list of policies and procedures. Instead, capitalize on their anticipation by handing them off to a team leader who will provide a tour and staff introductions.

Finish the day off with safety training or send them home a little early if you like. This way, they'll have sufficient time to digest everything they've learned and can mentally recharge their batteries for day two. Before the day is through, be sure to check in with the employee and your team to confirm who will be the point man for the second day of training.

ORIENTATION WEEK AND BEYOND

You may have noticed that I've stopped talking about your clone, and instead, have referred to a generic employee throughout this process. This was done intentionally to illustrate what every orientation should look like within your business. Nothing really changes with your clone, other than perhaps the amount of one-on-one coaching you'll be involved with.

The Employee Record should establish the right routines early on and set the pace for training. During the first week, it's important to keep your eyes and ears open and assess where improvements can be made, all while continuously checking in with your clone and building their confidence.

The subsequent weeks and months will follow a similar format, using their job description as a guide to set new goals, provide direction and lots of support. Don't hold them back and be clear that feedback goes both ways. If they have questions, concerns or need a refresher, then it's their responsibility to speak up. As their confidence and proficiencies grow, shift more accountability on to them and let go of the bike.

Chapter 22

SUPPORTING YOUR CLONE

Operating a vehicle has become second nature to experienced drivers, but for those who've never driven before, learning the new skill can be exciting, intimidating or even terrifying. In reality, their first time behind the wheel has little to do with their own abilities and everything to do with the person sitting beside them. A nurturing instructor will calm nerves and make for a pleasant experience, while an overbearing one could contribute to performance anxiety and costly mistakes.

Success in training can't be claimed by any one person – it's the combination of teamwork between the trainer, trainee, and co-workers. Too often, however, companies place the responsibility of learning a new job squarely on the shoulders of the employee, when really, this should be seen as a mutually-shared objective.

Supporting your clone means walking a fine line between control and freedom. On one side are the company's expectations which the employee must eventually comply with, and on the other, are the individual liberties needed for learning, creativity, and personalized service. Therefore, taking on a supporting role presents the challenge of maintaining equilibrium between the two until your clone is ready to fly on their own.

THE FEAR OF FEEDBACK

Feedback is an integral part of any training program, but for many people, the thought of giving or receiving it can be enough to send a chill down their spine. Some leaders feel uncomfortable providing feedback because it's awkward or they're afraid conflict will erupt at a moment's notice, while those on the receiving end find it embarrassing or downright insulting.

When you peel back the protective layers, you'll find everyone has the same insecurities and fears. We don't want to be perceived as lazy, incompetent, rude or be misrepresented in any other way by our actions. Often when feedback is given, one or both parties will tense up causing undue stress; but it doesn't have to be this way, and conversely, feedback should be seen as an opportunity to build up rather than tear down.

Building rapport with your clone (or any employee for that matter) is the secret to pain-free feedback. Open communication early in the relationship establishes trust, and trust encourages the free flow of ideas and opinions. The result is a safe learning environment where feedback is freely given and accepted in return, thus removing any social anxiety that would otherwise inhibit proper training.

TYPES OF FEEDBACK

We're all familiar with constructive criticism, or **Corrective Feedback** used to remedy problems and improve performance. This type of feedback gets the bad rap I mentioned earlier but through no fault of its own. In reality, any issues which arise usually stem from our approach rather than the process itself.

This circles back to our reactive nature when things don't go as planned. We instinctively tell somebody what not to do rather than instructing them how to proceed, leaving them confused and nervous about their next move. This is why, as trainers, we must be hyper aware that everything we say is clear and has value.

Additionally, we must also learn to maintain our poise when mistakes are made and accept the human error that comes with being human. Doing so will remove the reactionary element from the equation, enabling us to articulate the right information in a calm manner.

The second type of feedback is **Affirmative Feedback**, employed by leaders to reinforce positive behavior. This includes encouragement, recognition, and praise – all used to build their self-confidence and cultural buy-in.

An effective leader will utilize both feedback styles in equal parts and even layer them in a single delivery system for maximum results. These delivery systems can be either formal or informal in nature, depending on the situation at hand.

Informal Feedback is spontaneous in nature, usually in response to something experienced first hand. Informal affirmation could be a few words of inspiration or a pat on the back for a job well done. These are quick and easy ways to build habitual patterns and reinforce the fact that demonstrating the right behavior doesn't go unnoticed.

Informal corrective feedback is ideal for on-the-spot training, where improvements can be immediately communicated and accomplished with ease. A popular method to incorporate simultaneous corrective and affirmative feedback is the **Sandwich Technique**, where the constructive criticism is strategically placed between layers of positive reinforcement.

Say, for example, one of your employees is a well-known chatterbox and frequently visits with customers for an extended period of time. There's either too much schmoozing at the beginning of the interaction, or the conversation continues to drag on after the transaction is complete. The wrong approach would be to confront the employee and use inflammatory language, such as "I need you to get back to work" or "You're talking too much."

Despite your frustration, keep in mind that the employee likely has no idea there's a problem and believes visiting with customers is part of the job. To correct the behavior without rattling the cage, the sandwich technique looks something like this:

"It's great to see how well you're getting along with everyone."

" Just please be aware of how much time you're spending with each customer, and limit non-work related conversation to five minutes."

"Otherwise, great work!"

The corrective action remains the same, but this technique keeps difficult conversations professional without the hurt feelings.

Some people feel this is an outdated technique because it beats around the bush and dilutes the corrective message. I would argue the Sandwich Technique is still an effective feedback tool, but like everything else, you have to consider your audience.

I personally reserve this method for employees with shaky rapport or self-confidence. In these situations, I've found their sensitive nature increases the odds of an overreaction, so the additional compliments are a great way to feather everything out and maintain a constructive conversation. But once we have an open relationship and trust one another, I'll get right to the point because they know exactly where I'm coming from. As long as the recognition keeps coming in, the occasional critique is a welcomed opportunity for improvement.

As for **Formal Feedback**, these conversations are often pre-planned in advance and linked to either big picture objectives or more serious matters. Performance evaluations, regularly scheduled meetings and disciplinary hearings all fall into this category, where other factors such as setting and documentation must be taken into account.

SWITCH FEEDBACK

Confusion, insubordination, and disengagement are all tell-tale signs that an intervention may be required to get the employee back on track. But if you're uncomfortable with these types of conversations, it's easy to procrastinate and allow the situation to spiral out of control.

The **SWITCH Feedback Model** is your ticket to delivering a transformative message that improves the employee's performance without conflict. SWITCH stands for:

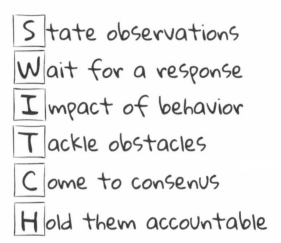

S tate observations
W ait for a response
I mpact of behavior
T ackle obstacles
C ome to consenus
H old them accountable

State Observations

Starting off with the right tone can be the difference between an intervention and an argument. It's always best to leave their attitude out of the equation and stick to the facts about their performance. Stating your observations opens the door to a discussion, while choosing inflammatory language simply gets their back up and reduces the chance of a civil resolution.

Here are a few examples of what <u>not</u> to say:

Don't say	Replace with...
"You're always late"	"Your timecard indicates you've been late twice this week"
"You have a bad attitude"	"I've noticed you haven't been yourself lately"
"Do I have to repeat myself?"	"We've had several conversations, and this appears to be a reoccurring problem"

Avoid asking questions which could open the door to an excuse. For instance, if you ask somebody why they were late, their response satisfies your question and marks the end of the conversation. However, if you take the perspective of an outside observer and state, "I noticed you were late," the subject casually shifts to performance standards, forcing the employee to justify their actions and acknowledge their behavior.

Wait for a Response

The easiest step also happens to be the most difficult. Silence is awkward, so we naturally try and fill the void by saying something – anything. After you've stated your observations, go silent and wait for them to reply. At first, they may look blankly back at you or give a one-word answer, say nothing. They may stall or lay a guilt trip on you, do not respond.

The only appropriate time to interject is when the talk begins to divert in another direction. When an employee's back is to the wall, their last-ditch effort is to bring others into the conversation and distribute the blame. In these circumstances only respond with, "Right now we're only talking about you," and then resume your silence.

The employee will feel the pressure, and they'll instinctively ramble on, fumbling over their words until they run out of things to say. Eventually, the truth will come out, and you can move on to the next step.

I would also like to point out that waiting for a response is an effective strategy to extract information for all sorts of scenarios. I employ this tactic all the time when I'm interviewing exceptionally shy individuals and want to get inside their head. It's also great for getting extra deals out of my vendors or playing chicken to see which one of us will budge and accept responsibility for a mishap.

It's a fantastic tool so use it, and use it often!

Impact of Behavior

With the spotlight placed on the employee, you're now ready to discuss the impact of their behavior. The objective here is to clear up any misunderstandings and have the employee take ownership of both the problem and solution for their performance.

Begin by asking them how their behavior impacts the company and again, wait for the right response. This is your check-mate move, which finally gets them to open up about what happened and why it's not ok. It's important they process their actions on their own before you chime in, because it's this acknowledgment which gets them on your side and cranks up their reception.

By now they're ready to listen to what you have to say, so it's the perfect time to revisit the Cultural Framework. Touch on the company's vision and values, then continue with whatever goals, standards or training will be used to reset the bar and measure their performance. In some ways, you're giving them the benefit of the doubt that their actions were a misunderstanding, but this is a one-off and moving forward, there's no question what must be done and why.

The final 10% of this conversation is consequence, and without it, you've essentially written a blank check for future inadequacies. Consequence can be anything from revoked privileges to more serious disciplinary action, but the point remains the same: for every action, there's a reaction, and it's the employee's duty to meet all company expectations moving forward.

Tackle Obstacles

Positioning yourself as a support system rather than an authoritative figurehead will enable you to work alongside the employee and improve their performance without raising their guard. In order for the employee to take ownership of the solution, they must identify what obstacles are in their way, determine the best course of action and commit to habitual change.

After you've laid everything on the line, the logical follow-up question to ask is, "What needs to be done to make this happen?" This will show the employee you're not out to get them and that you're actually on the same side. If they miss their mark or provide a single answer, continue to probe by asking "what else" to encourage their creativity. Forcing them to come up with multiple solutions will only strengthen your argument that the desired behavior can be accomplished in a number of ways, and they'll be more inclined to take action if it's their idea.

Afterward, you're free to include your own perspectives and suggestions to resolve the issue. It's also beneficial to re-evaluate your own methods to ensure they're receiving and interpreting the information correctly.

Come to a Consensus

The pivotal moment for change occurs when you come together to set a goal and agree on the resolution process. This consensus marks a new beginning and the time to repair any residual tension. If you express your appreciation and remind them you're in their corner, this should be enough to lift their spirits and get their head back into the game.

As for yourself, take a moment to appreciate their position and the challenges they face. Accept their shortcomings and don't hold any ill-will against them. If you're expecting them to turn over a new leaf than you should be prepared to do the same.

Hold Them Accountable

Remember that actions speak louder than words, so what you do in the coming days and weeks will either strengthen or weaken your brand. Reinforcing the right behavior early on will improve the odds for rehabilitation and reaffirm your commitment to improving their performance. Continue to follow-up until consistency has been achieved, and don't forget to celebrate their progress along the way.

COLLABORATION

There are all kinds of ways to support your clone and help them find their footing. My personal favorite is to collaborate on a project – nothing too extravagant to start out with, just something that will take a week or two. Working side-by-side is a great way to develop your relationship and catch a glimpse into the other person's world that would otherwise go unseen.

For example, you may observe:

- o How they structure their day and prioritize tasks

- o How they manage their stress and deal with difficult situations

- o Their creative and strategic processes

- o Previously unknown skills and interests

- o A completely new side to the person when their guard is lowered

The list goes on and on, and the benefits are tremendous. With a deeper understanding of what makes each other tick, your styles will steadily merge together as you both adapt your behavior to accommodate the other; and when this occurs, the true cloning process will be underway.

Bringing them into the planning stages will also provide numerous training opportunities that would otherwise be missed. You can bounce ideas off them, request feedback and share personal experiences. There may even be times where you can divide and conquer on the project, empowering your clone to take the lead with their own objectives and practice self-reliance.

Overtime, their confidence will build, and they'll have a pretty good idea of what to expect from you. After the project is complete, move on to another and then another, until you feel confident delegating permanent duties to your clone.

THE TRANSITION OF POWER

It's the big day, the moment of truth: your clone is about to step into their new role and take the reins for the first time. You've worked closely with them for a while now, and you're both on the same page. But what about the rest of your team? Have they been informed of what's going on and given adequate time to prepare, or are they about to be blindsided?

Supporting your clone means setting them up for success, which also includes a smooth transition of power. By smooth, I mean calm and quiet – business as usual. Best-case scenario; your clone is quickly accepted by the group, and everyone continues to do their job with minimal disruption. Sure, there may be an awkward adjustment period when the leader has less practical experience and must earn the respect of their team, but this is typically short-lived, and things will eventually return to normal.

As for the worst-case scenario, that entirely depends on your situation. Let's just say that overlooking this step is a recipe for disaster – even for companies with a healthy organizational culture. When employees are left in the dark, all sorts of bad things can happen, including:

- Confusion of who's in charge and the defined lines of jurisdiction
- Miscommunication, inefficiencies and avoidable mistakes
- Disagreements and gossip of who should be in charge
- An epidemic of panic and fear
- Resentment and hurt feelings
- Resistance to authority and sabotage
- Ultimatums and resignations

The list goes on and on, but you get the idea. It's impossible to say with certainty how others will react to the news, hence the need for a frank conversation beforehand. The keyword here is <u>before</u> – not soliciting feedback afterward or addressing concerns on the fly.

It's your responsibility as the Commander-in-Chief to not only empower leaders beneath you but also to establish the right environment for a fluid transition of power.

So how to do you bring everyone in on the plan and garner their support without opening a giant can of worms? One word: transparency.

Don't overthink this process because it's actually quite simple: get everyone who needs to know into a room, explain what's going on and why. That's it! There's no need to beat around the bush or sugarcoat the news. It worked for me, and it will work for you too.

My tone was light and upbeat so others would get excited instead of getting their back up. It's no secret that people fear change, unless of course that change directly benefits them. By addressing what was in it for them, I knew they'd be more receptive to my message and more inclined to get on board.

As for my message itself, I just framed the situation as a solution to a problem they were perhaps unaware of. I explained that the congestion of work funneling toward me was inhibiting everyone's ability to properly do their job and something had to change.

Again, I chose my wording carefully to ensure my employees didn't see themselves as the problem and immediately get defensive. I sold them on how everything would get better with somebody else at the front line, somebody who be more accessible to field questions and streamline decisions.

I also spread a little icing on top by forecasting less stress, improved efficiencies and additional opportunities for growth. To my surprise, my clone had nearly everyone's support right out of the gate – it was a win-win for everyone!

Remember, the best way to rally the troops is to communicate your vision for the future, so they have something to look forward to and get behind. Where do you envision the company a year or two from now, and what pivotal role with your clone play during this process?

The clarity and tone of your message should be enough to shift the group's attention away from petty office politics, or at the very least, create a platform where concerns can be addressed in a constructive manner. Either way, the transparency will squash speculation and rumors, enabling your clone to take charge with minimal resistance.

On a final note, I've found that a week's notice is usually sufficient for others to mentally prepare for this change. By then, emotions have subsided and the wrinkles ironed out, and after the weekend, everyone's ready to turn over a new leaf.

Meetings are another way to collaborate with your clone, and the final two chapters of this section will cover everything you need to know about them. We covered a lot in this chapter, so I encourage you to revisit it periodically to ensure your clone is receiving the highest quality of your support.

Chapter 23

TYPES OF MEETINGS

If you recall in Section One, I outlined a series of strategies to get out of meetings in an effort to protect your time. My intention wasn't to cast meetings in a negative light, but rather point out that as a leader you must recognize when you need to be involved and when you don't. In the right circumstances, meetings can be a powerful tool to streamline communication, improve workflow efficiencies and build team morale, but their overall effectiveness depends on your understanding and ability to facilitate them.

There are four types of meetings that belong in the leader's toolbox, each with a unique purpose and approach:

1. Daily Check-Ins

2. Weekly Roundtable Meetings

3. Strategic Meetings

4. Face-to-Face Meetings

DAILY CHECK-INS

These informal meetings last no more than ten minutes and are conducted periodically throughout the day as part of your regular duties. Daily check-ins are quick conversations between individuals or a small team to pass along information, receive updates, resolve minor issues, build team morale, and set the pace for the day.

But the benefits don't stop there. Industry leaders have found that replacing traditional performance reviews with more concise, on-the-spot feedback actually improves job satisfaction and productivity. Daily check-ins are also a time management godsend, because when your team expects to see you on a regular basis, they'll be more inclined to hold their questions instead of constantly disrupting you.

Supporting your clone means building their confidence and helping them reach their goals. One of the biggest mistakes you can make during your daily check-ins is to pull rank and undermine your clone's authority. Only in dire circumstances should you overrule their decisions; your goal is to make them look good and offer suggestions for improvement.

WEEKLY ROUNDTABLE MEETINGS

Once a week you should meet with your management team to discuss the day-to-day operations of the business. These meetings are kept to an hour with no more than a dozen people in attendance. A smaller group will always be more efficient because it takes less time to share ideas and make decisions.

Weekly meetings follow a regular itinerary covering the most relevant topics to your business, such as safety, sales, and marketing to name a few. The roundtable format is ideal for group collaboration and requires each person to prepare and participate in their own way. While some members hold facilitation duties like Chairperson and Secretary, everyone is still expected to bring certain things into the meeting and leave with newly appointed tasks.

This is also the best time to strengthen the group cohesion of your A-team. When your managers are telling stories, acknowledging wins, and collectively making decisions, what they're really doing is sharing the burden of responsibility and presenting a united front. As their trust in one another grows, so will their willingness to take the reins and work together to realize the company's vision.

Your encouragement is vital to keep this magic alive, and the easiest way to do so is to take a back seat and play a supporting role. Think of yourself as the facilitator to present topics for discussion and help cultivate ideas. Occasionally they may need to be reoriented in the right direction, but otherwise don't chime in until everyone else has spoken. Remember, the goal is to train your team to rely on each other instead of you.

STRATEGIC MEETINGS

As the name suggests, these meetings focus on strategic initiatives to realign the company's vision, mission and direction. Often billed as seminars, retreats and other names depending on their purpose, strategic meetings are conducted periodically throughout the year to dig deeper into critical issues and collaborate on long-term projects.

STAY FOCUSED!

Strategic meetings are best held outside of regular business hours or offsite to minimize outside distractions. Don't forget to put your phone in airplane mode as well!

This is commonly where opportunities and threats are examined to determine future marketing campaigns, financial forecasts, and budgets. Of course, not all strategic meetings are this heavy, and in many cases, they include team-building exercises to blow off steam and gain fresh perspectives.

FACE-TO-FACE MEETINGS

Sometimes meeting face-to-face makes the most sense, even if additional costs or inconveniences are involved. We rely on body language to express ourselves and navigate conversations, which is particularly helpful during formal progress meetings and training sessions. Your clone's facial expressions, posture, and gestures are all key indicators of how they're interpreting your message, signaling to go into more detail when they're reluctant to ask.

The personal attention that comes with face-to-face meetings is useful to build rapport and make others feel valued. As leaders, we can lose sight of what's really important and the impact we have on others. Whether you're thanking an employee for their service, providing specialized training or being a sounding board for their concerns, the time and attention you offer them will only strengthen your brand. Face-to-face meetings are a way to humanize yourself as a leader and enrich the quality of your service.

The informal nature of daily check-ins makes them the easiest ones to do, but formal meetings, on the other hand, can vary in complexity depending on the circumstances. As the stakes become higher, more variables come into play, and consequently, the increased need for structure. Let's continue the conversation in the next chapter, where I'll lay out the foundation for an award-winning meeting.

Chapter 24

RUNNING AN AWARD-WINNING MEETING

Meetings can be a worthwhile investment and bring huge value to both the company and its employees – when executed correctly. The problem, however, is that most leaders receive little to no training in this area when it's arguably just as important as any other leadership skill. So what happens? We get stuck in a bunch of bad meetings and continue to fall short of our goals, resulting in compounded frustration and discouragement.

You can continue down this path using trial and error if you have the stomach for it, or you can follow the **Eight-Step Proven Path to Run an Award-Winning Meeting**:

8 Simple Steps

1 Define Scope	**2** Create Itinerary	**3** Prepare For Meeting	**4** Begin Meeting
5 Facilitate Meeting	**6** End Meeting	**7** Follow Up	**8** Share & Celebrate

Step 1: Define the Scope of Meeting

The first step is to define your purpose, expectations and desired outcomes for the meeting. Together they should revolve around a central theme so the meeting feels like it's working toward an end result.

After establishing a clear direction, you can proceed to identify the other parameters of your meeting, including:

- o   When and where will the meeting take place?

- o   Who will be involved and how will they contribute?

- o   How formal or informal will the meeting be?

- o   Will the meeting be a regular occurrence?

Step 2: Create an Itinerary

An itinerary is more than just an outline of discussion points, it also includes the logistics surrounding the meeting itself. This step is more applicable to weekly and strategic meetings where additional organization is required to get everyone on the same page. For less formal or more intimate meetings, such as face-to-face, a simple outline of talking points would suffice.

You'll notice the top of the itinerary resembles a party invitation. The itinerary itself is meant to be distributed to all of the attendees with adequate notice so they can prepare for the meeting and adjust their schedules accordingly.

As for the **Meeting Information** and **Purpose**, this can simply be copied over from Step 1 after the scope of the meeting is defined.

Meeting Itinerary

Meeting Information

Date: Tuesday, May 5   Minutes Taker: _____

Time: 9:30 AM   Chairperson: _____

Location: Boardroom

Attendees:

Purpose

To review operational business for the upcoming week and follow up on outstanding items.

Agenda

I.   Old Business [5 Min]

II. Round Table Discussion: [40 Min]

    A. Safety

    B. Sales & Marketing

    C. Short-Term Projects, Opportunities & Initiatives

    D. Problems & Resolutions

    E. Other Business Relevant to the Group

III. Upcoming Events & Schedule Notifications [5 Min]

IV. Review Point Leads for Actionable Items [5 Min]

V.   Final Remarks [5 Min]

Meeting minutes will be distributed by: Friday, May 8th

The **Agenda** is the physical outline of the meeting's content and will vary depending on your purpose, goals, meeting format, and business. The items featured here are only an example, and your agenda could include presentations, group activities, training sessions, and anything else you can think of.

Here are a few points to consider when creating your own:

- o Indicate how much time will be allocated for each section. This will aid in the scheduling process and keep the meeting on track.

- o Begin and end the meeting with actionable items. Results are produced through delegation, follow-up and accountability – not conversation and luck.

- o Allow for some wiggle room so others can bring up additional points for discussion. But remember, if the conversation doesn't benefit the majority of the participants it should be benched for another time.

Include a memo at the bottom indicating when the minutes will be distributed. This is a final call to accountability for everyone to follow through on their responsibilities after the meeting has been adjourned.

TIME-WIZARD TIP!

Save yourself the hassle and download this template at www.jeffhilderman.com/resources

Step 3: Prepare for Meeting

Sitting through a long, unorganized meeting is torture, even when you're getting paid for it. Out of respect for your team's time (and sanity), make all of the necessary preparations in advance to keep things running smoothly. After the itinerary has been distributed to the other attendees, you'll need to supplement it with your own talking points. Know your facts, write them down and rehearse your presentation, so it's delivered in a professional manner.

Here's a list of additional items you may want to include in your checklist:

- ✓ Verify the availability of the venue and necessary equipment

- ✓ Arrange transportation and confirm logistics with additional presenters

- ✓ Make additional copies of the itinerary and other resources

- ✓ Bring props and stationery supplies

- ✓ Setup easel, laptop, audio/visual equipment and WIFI

- ✓ Have everything 100% setup and ready to go before anyone else arrives

- ✓ Bring coffee and snacks – not mandatory, but a nice touch!

Step 4: Begin the Meeting

We're all guilty of waiting for the stragglers to roll in while everyone else patiently waits and engages in meaningless chit-chat. Not surprisingly, this is the absolute <u>wrong</u> way to kick off a meeting, and allowing it to start even five minutes late immediately shaves off a layer of credibility to the meeting and its facilitator.

Meetings must always begin on time, even when others are running late. In these circumstances, it's not your job to be considerate, but rather, to set the tone for a productive meeting and signal that time-wasters will not be tolerated. Greet everyone with a warm welcome, skip the small talk, and jump right in.

Depending on the meeting's size, formality, and objectives, you may want to consider an ice breaker activity to get the group's creative and social juices flowing. A quick search on the internet can yield all sorts of ideas, ranging from sharing a personal story to interactive team-building activities. If you elect to go this route, choose an activity compatible with the theme of the meeting so you can naturally segue into your first point of discussion.

Step 5: Facilitate the Meeting

After the meeting is in full-swing, watch the time for each section and allow for a few minutes of wiggle room. If necessary, circle back to the topic or continue the conversation outside of the meeting if it doesn't concern the entire group. You'll often find a brief intermission will bring about more clarity than talking something to death.

But there's more to running an effective meeting than simply sticking to a schedule, it's also about creating the right climate where individualism and collaboration coexist. A consensus is rarely reached because everyone was on the same page from the get-go, and instead, is the byproduct of debate. As the facilitator, it's your responsibility to manage the chaos in a constructive manner and guide everyone toward resolution.

Follow these tips to keep the meeting moving in the right direction:

- Establish a code of conduct up front to preserve the integrity of the meeting and ensure everyone is treated respectfully.

- Praise publicly, critique privately. Create a safe space where it's ok to speak up, voice concerns and share ideas without persecution.

- Everyone has a perspective and a potentially great idea. Engage everyone equally and don't allow certain individuals to steamroll over the group.

- There's a difference between disagreement and criticism. The tone of the meeting should remain positive at all times.

- Don't accept excuses and ask as many follow questions as necessary to get to the underlying issue.

- Ask an open-ended question to make everyone think, and play the devil's advocate to encourage conversation.

- Always be the last one to state your opinion.

- Solicit feedback before moving on to the next topic to ensure everyone's on the same page.

- Take notes, record decisions and appoint leads on actionable items.

- For strategic meetings or seminars which exceed two hours, allow for brief intermission to recapture the group's attention.

Step 6: End the Meeting

All effective meetings end on a high note, even if the journey to get there was mentally draining. It's important your team walks away feeling appreciated and inspired to take action, otherwise, the meeting was just a waste of everyone's time. Wrap it up with a positive message, a funny story or simply a heartfelt thank you. Don't forget to reiterate the main takeaways and course of action beforehand, to ensure the momentum continues after everyone goes their separate ways.

And finally, signal the meeting is over by being the first to stand up. This natural cue will invoke a chain reaction and enable you to promptly exit without getting sucked into post-meeting chatter.

Step 7: Follow Up on Actionable Items

Stepping into the boardroom (or wherever your meetings take place) is like passing through a mirror into an augmented reality. It's easy to theorize how things will play out and come up with initiatives in a group setting, but it's a whole other ball game when you're back at your desk and bombarded with work.

What seemed like a priority an hour ago can quickly move to the back burner and remain there indefinitely without some sort of accountability. Get into the habit of following up with your team within 48 hours to keep their feet to the fire and help them get back on track while the priority still seems relevant. This is just an informal check-in meeting we covered earlier, nothing more and nothing less.

Step 8: Share Minutes and Celebrate Wins

Although meetings generally increase in efficiency with fewer people, this doesn't mean everyone else should be left in the dark. Whether you post the minutes in the staffroom or distribute them in a company newsletter, creating transparency is an essential component of staff engagement.

The more your employees know what's going on and the direction the company is headed, the more inclined they'll be to ask questions, offer suggestions, and understand how their contributions can make a difference. Likewise, it's equally important to celebrate individual accomplishments to remind everyone that the company's success is the accumulation of everyone's hard work.

BACK TO YOUR CLONE

So at this point, you may be wondering how any of this applies to supporting your clone, and the answer is two-fold. While the 8-step procedure was written in the context of a group setting, the rules apply to one-on-one meetings as well. Making the most out of your time together will accelerate their learning, and consequently, their capabilities to assume your duties.

Secondly, running effective meetings is a required skill set for all leaders. By improving your own skills at the same time as developing theirs, both of you will be able to lead effective meetings interchangeably with the same level of proficiency and confidence.

* * *

Big congratulations are in order because you've just completed the third section of this program! By now your clone should understand the company's Cultural Framework and the role they'll play to fulfill your vision. Understandably, all of this will take time before they're ready to venture out on their own, which is what the final thirty days are all about.

Section Four is dedicated to setting goals, monitoring their progress, and preparing your clone to leave the nest. It's the final piece of the puzzle, and frankly, the most satisfying part of the process. Everything you've worked for comes down to this, and soon you'll be ready to take flight yourself.

Section Four

LETTING GO

Chapter 25

PROGRESS MEETINGS

If you've ever watched professional racing like NASCAR or Formula 1, you'll know the drivers are world-class, and their vehicles are on the cutting edge of technology. But even the most skilled driver in the most expensive car can't get across the finish line without routinely pulling in for a pit stop. Although the deviation incurs a time penalty and disrupts the driver's work, they understand that refueling, new tires, and mechanical adjustments are all required to finish the race.

Employee training is very much like competitive racing. Your clone is given a car (their job), shown how to drive (training), and then pointed in the right direction (empowerment). It might take them a few laps to get a feel for the car and course, but eventually, they'll pick up speed and improve their performance. Sounds great, but what about the pit stops?

Just as their car needs fuel and maintenance, so too does your clone in the form of affirmative and constructive feedback. Regularly scheduled progress meetings allow you to temporarily pull them off the track to review their accomplishments, provide guidance, field questions, and set new goals together.

The frequency of these meetings will depend on your clone's previous experience and proficiency after the first thirty days, but the general rule of thumb is to conduct three consecutive monthly meetings and then move to quarterly thereafter.

THE GOOD, THE BAD AND THE NECESSARY

Daily check-ins may reign supreme as the most effective type of meeting, but their informal and versatile nature inhibit deep conversations from taking place. Progress meetings, on the other hand, present a unique opportunity to string all

PROGRESS MEETINGS   179

of the big picture stuff together, including your clone's own experiences and perspectives. This will be sacred bonding time that both of you look forward to, openly communicating and sharing ideas first as mentor and student, and then, eventually, as equals.

Progress meetings are not personal evaluations or catch up sessions. They are more meaningful conversations which address the *why* behind your feedback, connecting the dots between your clone's actions and the company's ideologies. And it's this connection that bridges the gap between what they are told and what they believe, necessary for them to buy into the culture and fully understand their role. As for the conversation itself, there are some specific things which need to be discussed.

The Good is everything they're doing right, including the skills they've learned and improved, the proper behaviors they've exhibited and how well they interact with others. It's also the time to recognize their progress, the challenges they've overcome and how their contributions have made a difference.

The intent is to make them feel comfortable early on in the meeting, build their confidence and commend them on a job well done. But don't forget about the *why*, which takes the conversation to the next level. Be sure to include the significance of their personal brand and how they must lead by example.

The Bad isn't actually bad, it's just about establishing a safe environment where concerns can be discussed. Obviously, you'll want to address their areas of improvement, but the real objective is to get your clone to open up about their own silent struggles.

Perhaps they're confused about something that was said or done and were too shy to seek clarification at the time. Maybe they're uncomfortable with a certain portion of their job and require additional training. There may also be other factors at play that you're completely unaware of, such as a learning disability or medical issue. Whatever obstacles are uncovered, demonstrate empathy toward your clone and reassure them you'll work through all of it together.

The theme of the conversation should remain upbeat and constructive, even when tough discussions take place. If there's a problem with their performance, take the time to explain why the change is necessary and refer back to the Cultural Framework. The transparency will develop the trust in your relationship and strengthen your rapport.

The Necessary is everything else to make the dialog feel like a natural conversation instead of a probationary hearing. This includes the solicitation of their opinions, fielding questions, setting goals, sharing observations, and personal antidotes. When your clone feels comfortable in the meeting, they'll be more inclined to tell you what's really on their mind. Likewise, the more interested you appear in what they have to say, the more receptive they'll be to your feedback.

THE MEETING

Progress meetings follow the face-to-face format we discussed earlier, so let's go into the finer details of how to prepare and conduct this meeting to ensure you hit the first one out of the park.

The Itinerary

With the scope defined, you can immediately proceed to the preparation of the itinerary. **There are four specific conversations that will take place during your meeting**, so the itinerary must be structured in a way that one naturally flows into the next.

The first topic addresses **their progress thus far**, covering anything and everything that comes to mind. After the initial meeting, this will also be the right time to review any previously established goals.

The next step is to **tie the conversation into the bigger picture** as they relate their personal experiences to the Cultural Framework. Ask them to recite the company's vision, mission, and mantra if they can, and provide an explanation of what it means to them. They should draw on previous experiences, give examples, and state what they believe.

The third conversation is where you and your clone will **set goals together**. Review their job description and come up with an action plan for the next thirty days: determine what's doable, what's required, and what's optional. Providing a few options to choose from is a subtle way to establish accountability early on and make them feel like they're in control of their own destiny.

After you've reviewed their performance, linked it to the bigger picture, and set goals together, the final conversation takes aim at their **personal development**. An introductory training session may be appropriate if time permits, otherwise, arrange another face-to-face meeting for another time. For example, if your clone is ready to take on a leadership role, they must be first taught the fundamentals such as prioritization, delegation, and follow up.

Progress Report

Name: _____   Date: _____

Date (Last Meeting): _____

Agenda _____

1. Recap Since Last Report (Employee, You)

    a. Overall Impression   b. Accomplishments

    c. Challenges / Obstacles / Concerns   d. Review Previous Goals

2. Review Cultural Framework & Personal Experiences (Employee, You)

    a. Vision & Mission   b. Core Values

    c. Standards & Guidelines   d. Personal Brand

3. Review Job Description (Employee, You)

    a. Previous Duties & Goals   b. Field Questions

    c. Set Goals for Next 30 Days   d. Employee Feedback

4. Personal Development (Employee, You)

    a. Leadership Qualities   b. Delegation & Follow Up

    c. Providing Feedback   d. Time Management

5. Final Remarks (Employee, You)

Bite Your Tongue!

You'll notice beside each header is listed (Employee, You). This is your visual reminder to let them do the talking first, but we'll go more into that in a moment.

TIME-WIZARD TIP!

Save yourself the hassle and download this template at www.jeffhilderman.com/resources

The good news is that once your itinerary is created, it can be reused for every subsequent progress meeting. Even though the structure is the same, each meeting will take place on a higher level as your clone becomes closer to becoming your equal.

Preparation

A progress meeting isn't the sort of thing you want to spring on your clone, especially when you're looking for genuine, well thought-out answers. Be sure to give them a copy of the itinerary a few days in advance, so they have adequate time to prepare. They can jot down anything that comes to mind throughout the day, but their actual write-up should be conducted at home when they have a clear mind and are free from distractions.

WARNING, HAZARD AHEAD!

Don't make the mistake of handing your clone a piece of paper and assuming they'll know what to do. Explain the purpose of the meeting and the sorts of answers you're looking for, including a disclaimer that single-word answers will not suffice.

Your preparation is conducted in a similar fashion, but there's an additional step involved. As you observe them performing their duties, take note of their personal behaviors and mannerisms. Are they outgoing, loud, relaxed, timid, quiet, or nervous? Do they feel comfortable asking questions and writing things down? Will they extend a helping hand without being asked or do they need to be prodded?

These are the immeasurable actions which often go unnoticed, and studying them will allow you to step into their shoes and get inside their head. If you can anticipate how they're thinking and feeling going into the meeting, you'll have a better idea of how it will play out and prepare for it accordingly.

For example, if you sense they're self-conscious, prepare a brief uplifting message in advance. If they're making lots of mistakes, you might be able to call them out on not asking enough questions or writing things down.

The point is, don't go into the meeting cold; have an idea of what you're going to say, imagine their response and then craft yours. This will also be beneficial for scenarios where your clone isn't opening up or engaging in a two-way conversation. Throw a little bait on the table to get them talking, whether it's a challenge you believe they're facing or an accomplishment they're proud of.

Conducting the Meeting

Your first progress meeting will always be a little rocky compared to the ones that follow, but there are a few things you can do to ease the awkwardness. You'll first need to create a comfortable, supportive environment conducive to sharing. Establish a few casual ground rules for your clone at the beginning of the meeting, such as:

- o "Be 100% honest and don't hold back anything you want to say."

- o "Don't say anything you think I want to hear. I only want your personal opinion."

- o "Ask lots of questions. If there's anything I say that's unclear, please let me know."

Take a moment to reiterate the purpose of the meeting and how you're looking forward to what they have to say, then wrap up the introduction with a few words of appreciation.

Another way to ease their anxiety is to inject humor when appropriate, but only if you can do this naturally without it coming off as premeditated. Alternatively, sprinkle compliments throughout the meeting as a way to build them up and keep them focused on what you have to say.

As you go into the meeting, remember you're there to serve. You've created a unique opportunity for both of you to better understand one another, and so the tone of the meeting must match its purpose. Seek clarification, provide guidance, nurture their emotions and build them up, all while maintaining a neutral tone as if two friends were chatting over coffee.

I'll admit that I'm terrible for cutting people off mid-sentence. I've certainly got better over the years, but it's one of my flaws, and I know it. It sickens me to think how many ideas and opinions I've unintentionally squashed because of my impatience. Furthermore, when I told somebody I was interested in what they had to say, and then immediately shut them down, you can bet that hurt my leadership brand.

One of the most crucial things you can do in the progress meeting is to let them do most of the talking. Begin each conversation with a few open-ended questions which can't be responded with a yes or no, and then keep your mouth shut. It's ok once and a while to interject with an acknowledgment or steer the conversation back on track if you have to, but keep the disruptions to an absolute minimum. Once your clone has said their peace, you can dive into any follow-up questions and proceed with your own points.

It should go without saying, but also take lots of notes! There will be many great points brought up that you'll want to record and refer back to a later time. This is especially important when you're setting goals so they can be followed up soon after and revisited at the next progress meeting.

As the meeting draws to a close, recap your action plan and remember to end on a high note with a few words of encouragement and a thank you.

Follow Up and Celebrate Wins

There's a small window of opportunity in the days following the meeting to capitalize on your clone's peaked levels of receptiveness and engagement. If possible, compile and review the meeting minutes with your clone the next day and jump right into the newly established goals. During this time, they'll be reeling from the effects of the progress meeting and be more likely to ask questions and offer feedback. Keep this as part of your daily check-ins and look for opportunities to recognize their accomplishments.

Goals are only as good as the results they produce, which is why I've dedicated an entire chapter on how to set them correctly. There's no slowing down now, so let's keep going.

Chapter 26

SETTING GOALS

By now we can all agree that goal-setting is important, but what we haven't covered is how to do it correctly. In Chapter 2, I used New Year resolutions as an example to illustrate the relationship between motivation and accomplishing your goals. It's true that your mindset plays a significant role in long-term success, but is it enough to produce the right results? Not exactly.

You might have a great attitude as you study for an exam, but failure to get all of your work done on time could have disastrous consequences. Similarly, anyone who sets unrealistic goals for themselves to lose weight or save money will, inevitably, be left disappointed regardless of how hard they work.

Proper goal-setting is the link between your will to achieve something and the ability to do it. You might eventually figure it out or barely scrape by, but there are no guarantees unless you know the right way to set goals and make them stick.

SMART GOALS

SMART has been around since the early 80's and has become the go-to model for setting goals of all types and sizes. The system was originally developed by George T. Doran as a way to establish clear and reachable goals, and since then, has been studied extensively and altered to become different things to different people. Even more impressive is the fact that the core principles introduced nearly four decades ago remain just as relevant today.

The most common interpretation of SMART is that effective goals must be **Specific, Measurable, Achievable, Relevant** and **Timebound**.

Specific

Goals must be clear and definitive, otherwise, you'll struggle to find the right course of action or lack the motivation to achieve them. Once you've drafted your goal run it through the 5W Test to ensure it's specific enough:

- o **What** do I want to accomplish?

- o **Why** am I doing it?

- o **Where** will it take place?

- o **Who** will be involved?

- o **Which** tools do I need to be successful?

Example:

Imagine you wanted to improve the customer service in your business. Your goal could be to develop a new employee training program for your business, using the latest strategies and technologies, to improve the customer experience.

Measurable

Having tangible results are essential for monitoring progress, meeting deadlines and keeping yourself motivated along the way. Measurable goals define the end result and answer the fundamental question, "How will I know when I'm finished?"

Example:

Before you can create a new training program, you must first identify the criteria needed to improve the customer's experience. This could include greeting customers with a smile, answering the phone by the second ring, and resolving issues on the spot.

Achievable

Goals can be ambitious, but they also have to be 100% attainable, otherwise, you're just planning to fail. Another common pitfall to avoid is hedging your bets against outside factors you don't have direct control over like the weather or economy. It's a fool's game to gamble with your goals, so stick to the path of certainty and continue to build on them once you gain traction.

Example:

If the organizational culture is unhealthy in your business, it's unrealistic to expect everyone will immediately buy into the new training program and do an about-face on their performance. Therefore, setting a goal to meet your criteria in six months may be realistic, while achieving it in thirty days probably isn't.

Relevant

Do your goals matter and are they aligned with the bigger picture? If not, you might be wasting your time and resources. When setting goals in business, for example, it's essential they run parallel with the organization's vision, mission, and values and will propel the company forward in some meaningful way. If the relevancy of your goal is in question, revisit the specific purpose to give it new meaning or, perhaps, set it aside for another time.

Example:

Do the criteria in your training program actually improve the customer's experience and is it aligned with your vision? If your values include honesty and integrity and your new salesmanship tactics are sleazy, you're going to have a serious conflict of interest. Or if you're training your team to do things your customers place little to no value on, you'll be banging your head against the wall when you don't see the return on your investment.

TimeBound

Without a deadline, there's no accountability or motivation to stay on course. Timebound goals prevent daily tasks from taking priority over your long-term goals and keep the finish line in view.

Example:

Creating and implementing a training program is going to take time, whether you're doing it yourself or delegating it to somebody else. If the project seems somewhat overwhelming, you could break it down into bite-sized pieces and set a deadline for each component to be created, reviewed, and finalized. Most importantly, create a deadline to implement the program and another to benchmark its effectiveness.

USING SMART GOALS

Progress meetings are an opportune time to discuss and set SMART goals with your clone. Whether you're reviewing new duties from their job description or addressing specific areas of improvement, SMART goals are a natural and effective way to plan for future success.

Allocate ten or fifteen minutes at the end of the meeting to review this process with your clone, and then encourage them to verbally make several goals based on the action plan moving forward. Effective goal-setting is an essential skill in the leadership toolbox, and the earlier your clone learns how to appropriately set goals, the faster they'll pick everything else up.

It's also worth mentioning that goal-setting doesn't stop once your clone is at the helm; if anything, your goals should become more ambitious now that you have somebody else to help you accomplish them.

It's always amusing to review my old notebooks from ten years ago and compare my goals back then to those I make today. Back then I didn't look more than a month or two into the future, and I would perhaps set one audacious goal each year.

Here are a few examples of what I had written down:

- o *Create new special order policy*
- o *Review safety checklist for new employees*
- o *Update approved uniform list*
- o *Create manager job description*
- o *Increase sales by 10%*

Pretty sad, isn't it? Obviously, these goals don't fit the SMART criteria, but they're also very short-sighted and more closely resemble daily tasks. This is what living day-to-day or month-to-month looks like. There's nothing to look forward to, nothing exciting or ambitious that will propel the company forward.

I'm happy to report that my goals today look quite a bit different. I'm strategically planning for five and tens years down the road, which includes a specific roadmap to get there. I review my goals monthly instead of annually, which allows me to tackle bite-sized objectives and take the necessary corrective action to stay on track.

This is precisely why I'm an advocate for cloning yourself. By putting somebody else in charge of the present, you can effectively turn your attention to the future and set new goals for yourself. So dare to dream big, and don't forget to wave to everyone after you cross the finish line.

Chapter 27

EMPOWERING YOUR CLONE

Handing control over to your clone is the final step of BASIC Training and the contents of this program, with the mandate of developing the street-smarts every leader needs to survive in the real world. Theories, step-by-step guides, and case studies are all excellent learning tools, but the actual development of these skills, and the ability to adapt to unexpected circumstances rely on practical, hands-on experience.

With the first progress meeting behind them and a new set of goals to look forward to, the time has finally come for your clone to venture out on their own. Don't worry, this doesn't mean the formal training period is over.

Your clone (and you) might be a little nervous at the prospect of flying solo, but think of it this way: the only way they'll ever learn how to perform under pressure is to figure things out on their own when they don't have answers. This is the street-smarts we're talking about, and it can't be taught in the classroom. After all, it's what got you here today, and is a rite of passage every leader must endure.

To be clear, I'm not talking about abandoning your clone and forcing them to fend for themselves. Instead, your clone must be strategically empowered to solve problems and take responsibility for their own goals. You'll still be there every step along the way to guide and nurture them, but at an arm's length and sometimes out of view.

LET THEM LEAD

Leaders can operate their teams one of two ways. The first approach is to withhold trust and individual responsibility by keeping all of the cards close to their chest and issuing commands on a need-to-know basis. The system works, but it comes with the price of owning every problem and controlling a disengaged workforce.

Alternatively, they can empower their team to take the initiative, encourage creativity and nurture personal development. This method involves everyone with the end product, not just the process, allowing the operation to run smoothly with greater efficiency and minimal supervision.

After their first thirty days, your clone should have a pretty good idea of what to expect from the company and you as their mentor. With the foundation laid and a new destination ahead, there's no reason why you should still be holding their hand. Your clone should be encouraged to plan their own day, prioritize tasks, solve problems, and try new things– even if it's not your way of doing it. They'll surprise you or they won't, but either way, they'll learn valuable lessons and carve a path on their own terms.

The same holds true for giving them the necessary space to discover who they are as a leader. Cloning yourself is about preserving the ideologies of the company and getting the same results, but the mechanics between A and B should be of little concern. Telling your clone exactly what to do and how to do it isn't empowerment, and it will deter both their innovation and engagement if not used sparingly. For now, give them lots of room to experiment with their leadership style and figure out what works – there will be plenty of time later on to refine their skills and mold their brand.

One of the greatest challenges I faced throughout the entire cloning process was giving my clone the appropriate space to learn and do their job. I instinctively offered suggestions instead of allowing them to figure out their own solutions. I tried to protect them from making the same mistakes I did instead of waiting to see how the situation would play out. Of course in my mind, I felt like I was empowering them, but I really wasn't. I was so concerned about their safety that I forgot (or subconsciously refused) to let go.

It all worked out after a while, and I eventually figured out that empowering my clone meant teaching them how to think and feel, instead of how to act. It took discipline to step back, watch them screw things up and dig themselves out of a hole. Sometimes I offered advice afterward and sometimes I didn't, unless they came to me with their tail between their legs.

My clone also realized they couldn't get a quick answer out of me anymore; if they wanted my opinion, they'd first have to walk me through their thought process from start to finish. Slowly but surely, my clone understood what it meant to be a leader, and I understood what it meant to be a mentor.

There are all sorts of ways you can let your clone take the lead:

- o   Transfer new responsibilities to your clone after every progress meeting
- o   Encourage them to set personal goals in addition to the ones set together
- o   Solicit their opinions and let them make decisions
- o   Bounce your own ideas off of them and request their feedback
- o   Include them in projects and assign meaningful responsibilities
- o   Have your clone facilitate parts of the weekly management meeting, and eventually act as Chairperson.
- o   Have them sit in on other face-to-face meetings when appropriate
- o   Include them on the financial side of the business. Show them where ground has been gained and lost so they can appreciate the real-life implications of their decisions

Letting go can be tough, especially for entrepreneurs who've grown accustomed to operating in the trenches. It's a double-edged sword because you want everything done a certain way at a certain speed, but you also recognize the pitfalls of being the bottleneck of your business.

Letting your clone lead is the act of letting go, and the entire premise of this book. It's inevitable that operations will slow down, mistakes will be made and your patience will be tested– but this comes with the territory of optimizing your business and freeing yourself up for more important matters. After you've empowered your clone to take the lead, **you must put your trust in them and step into your new role as a mentor.**

BE A RESOURCE

Make no mistake, being a resource to your clone is not planning out their day and spoon-feeding them answers. In many cases, it's just a matter of being a sounding board so they can work through solutions out loud and receive your stamp of approval. In the beginning, you can expect to play a very active mentoring role, offering continuous support through direct supervision and feedback. But over time, as their skills develop and their confidence grows, they'll be less concerned with seeking your approval and more focused on leading their team.

There will also be a gradual shift away from the company's operations and toward your clone's personal development. They will need your assistance to become a better communicator, organizer, trainer, and so on. Help them with their leadership brand, offer suggestions and role-play scenarios with them during your progress meetings.

Being a resource means sharing your experiences with them and teaching them everything you've learned– including the strategies in this book. You're a wealth of knowledge and have so much to give, so use your time wisely to put the finishing touches on your clone. Eventually, you'll get through the turbulence of training and the business will begin to coast on auto-pilot.

* * *

Phew! So how are you feeling right now? Excited, exhausted, overwhelmed, relieved, all of the above? Crossing the finish line means different things to different people, but above all else, you should feel proud of what you've accomplished. Going through the mental and physical transformation in just ninety days is no small feat, especially when you throw a second person into the mix.

But you did it! You achieved a level of success that most entrepreneurs only dream of, and proven to yourself that anything is possible. So now the only question remaining is where will you go from here?

Section Five

IGNITING YOUR PASSION

NOW'S YOUR TIME TO SHINE

We've reached the end of the cloning process, but your journey is far from over. There's always another mountain to climb and new adventures to be had; after all, you are an entrepreneur! Your company is in good hands, and for the first time in a long time, you have the freedom to pursue your passion.

While you've certainly earned the right to sit back and enjoy the fruit of your labor, understand there's still a fine line to walk within the first year of transition. Your clone will continue to seek your councel as they move through unchartered territory, but unless you fill your day with new, meaningful things, you could easily relapse and find yourself meddling in their affairs.

TAKE NOTE, FOUNDERS!

You top the list of high-risk offenders because this transition is hardest on you! You've endured the most sacrifice and hardship building your business, so letting go can bring about additional feelings of loss or regret.

Conversely, it's just as easy to go the other way and lose touch with your business. Stay informed, even just on the financial end, and devote the rest of your time to where it matters most for you.

SO, WHAT'S NEXT?

At last, you can remove your dream job description from the wall and work toward your new vision. Take a moment to review your goals and determine if they're still relevant. If you know exactly where your next path will take you then, by all means, carry on. If you need to reconsider your options, that's ok too.

Trust your instincts but don't shy away from lofty goals. Remember, what seemed like a monumental task only a few months ago is now behind you, and to quote Walt Disney, "If you can dream it, you can do it."

It's easier to take a neutral perspective and step into your customers' shoes when you're removed from the day-to-day operations of the business. What are your customers wants and needs, and how can you improve their overall experience? New products and services are a great place to start, but you'll need to think a bigger game if you're looking for exponential growth.

My father-in-law always said, "When you're unique, you have no competition," and it's the truth. Price wars, market share, it's all noise. If you really want to scale your company, just focus on your team and the end user experience – everything else will fall into place. Set the bar higher and higher until it's impossible for others to keep pace, and eventually, you'll find yourself in a league of your own.

The good news is that your experience and availability are conducive to your new role as **Chief Visionary Officer**. You can personally oversee the projects you want and delegate everything to your clone. You can work alongside them and continue to develop their leadership brand. Heck, you can even reapply the cloning process again and again to build an army!

Chapter 29

YOU CAN DO THIS

I wrote this book for every entrepreneur who has become their own best employee and the bottleneck of their business; for those unable to reap the rewards they deserve, and for anyone whose passion has been overshadowed by frustration and despair.

I wrote this book to open new doors of opportunity for you, at a time when it perhaps doesn't seem possible. I share my experiences because I'm living proof that you don't have to burn the candle at both ends to achieve your dreams.

Not too long ago I stood exactly where you stand now. I worked crazy hours at the expense of my personal life and health. My days were filled with agonizing moments of stupidity and frustration. I came home many nights feeling miserable and stressed out – completely dumbfounded with how to get myself out of this mess.

Then I began to apply the strategies in this book, and things gradually got better. I was no longer anchored down with *work,* which prevented me from doing my *job*. I gained laser-sharp focus, enabling me to carefully plan my next move and execute it with precision.

I finally felt in control of my ship and had a crew who could stay a step or two ahead of me. I also rediscovered my passion for helping people and inspiring them to do great things.

This book is my physical proof that the system works. I wake up every morning energized and with a sense of purpose. I'm doing the work I was meant to do, but I'm also home for dinner every evening. I play with my kids and tuck them into bed each night. We go on spontaneous road trips and have lazy days in our pajamas. Life is good, and it's all about balance.

Now it's your turn. This is your playbook to regain control of your business and help others help you realize your vision. This isn't a book meant to be read once and thrown in the pile with the others. Keep it handy, make notes and refer to it often. Share it with your team and anyone else who could use a little help.

Most importantly, take action. Make the decision right now to move forward and commit to change; not just at work, but in every aspect of your life.

Stop worrying about what others think and focus on what makes you happy. Get involved with your community and donate your time to somebody else in need. Build deeper relationships with your friends and family, travel, exercise or take up a new hobby. Who knows, maybe there's a book inside of you waiting to be written.

Just don't let life pass you by and remember to take care of yourself along the way, because even though you have a clone, there's still only one of you.

ALL-STAR ACADEMY: THE BIGGER PICTURE

I created All-Star Academy with one goal in mind: to help entrepreneurs build a business and a life they love.

The path may be long and not always clear, but one thing is certain: you do not have to travel it alone. All-Star Academy is an online community where entrepreneurs learn how to build their dream team, ask questions, share ideas, and support one another along the way.

If you think you could use additional support throughout your journey, I encourage you to join our community. We'd love to have you!

 For more information about the All-Star Community, check us out at: www.jeffhilderman.com

Whether you choose to join the ranks of All-Star Academy or not, I'd love to hear your accomplishments. When you complete the program, I hope you'll tell me about your business, your dream team, and how it has impacted your life.

You can reach me at jeff@jeffhilderman.com.

I hope to hear from you soon, and here's to a future of endless possibilities.

~ Jeff

RESOURCES

Lally, P., van Jaarsveld, C. H. M., Potts, H. W. W. and Wardle, J. (2010), How are habits formed: Modelling habit formation in the real world. Eur. J. Soc. Psychol., 40: 998-1009. doi:10.1002/ejsp.674. Accessed October 2, 2016. http://onlinelibrary.wiley.com/doi/10.1002/ejsp.674/abstract

Kasowski, Bart and Louise Jacques Filion. "A Study of the 2005 Fortune 500 Vision Statements." HEC Montréal, 2010. Accessed July 9, 2016. http://expertise.hec.ca/chaire_entrepreneuriat/wp-content/uploads/2010-04-cahier-vision-fortune-500.pdf

Wikipedia. "Southwest Airlines." Accessed October 30, 2016. https://en.wikipedia.org/wiki/Southwest_Airlines.

2011 Southwest Airlines One Report. "Principles of Living the Southwest Way." Accessed October 30, 2016. http://www.south westonereport.com/2011/#!/people/employees/one-luv.

Wall Street Journal Blog, The. "Google's 'Don't' Be Evil' Becomes Alphabet's 'Do the Right Thing'. Accessed November 15, 2016. https://blogs.wsj.com/digits/2015/10/02/as-google-becomes-alphabet-dont-be-evil-vanishes/.

Theme Park Tourist. "17 Mind-Boggling Statistics About the Disneyland Resort". Accessed December 30, 2016. http://www.themepark tourist.com/features/20140227/16405/17-mind-boggling-statistics-about-disneyland-resort.

Statistics Canada. "Unemployment Rates in Alberta and Canada." Accessed May 8, 2017. http://www.statcan.gc.ca/daily-quotidien/160205/cg-a003-eng.htm

THANKS FOR READING

I NEED YOUR HELP!

I love hearing success stories and would appreciate your feedback to make the next version of this book even better.

Please leave a helpful review on Amazon and share this book with anyone else who could use it.

Thanks again!

~ Jeff Hilderman